IMAGES
of Sports

THE ORANGEMEN
SYRACUSE UNIVERSITY
MEN'S BASKETBALL

FRED LEWIS AND DAVE BING. Fred Lewis poses with his first and most significant recruit, Dave Bing. Lewis assumed the head coaching duties at Syracuse in the spring of 1962. He immediately recruited Bing, a standout at Washington, D.C.'s Spingarn High School. Bing, pictured here in his senior year, helped Lewis turn the moribund program around.

IMAGES
of Sports

THE ORANGEMEN
SYRACUSE UNIVERSITY
MEN'S BASKETBALL

Mike Waters

ARCADIA
PUBLISHING

Published by Arcadia Publishing
Charleston SC, Chicago IL, Portsmouth NH, San Francisco CA

Printed in the United States of America

Library of Congress Catalog Card Number: 2003111356

For all general information contact Arcadia Publishing at:
Telephone 843-853-2070
Fax 843-853-0044
E-mail sales@arcadiapublishing.com
For customer service and orders:
Toll-Free 1-888-313-2665

Visit us on the Internet at www.arcadiapublishing.com

A TEAM OF LEGENDS. The 1955–1956 Orangemen had a modest 14-8 record, but the team included future All-American Vince Cohen and football legend Jim Brown. Cohen is in the front row on the far right. Brown is in the back row, third from the right. The head coach, Marc Guley, is in the back row on the far left.

CONTENTS

ACKNOWLEDGMENTS

I first want to thank Tiffany Howe and Amy Sutton at Arcadia Publishing for making this book happen. I would like to thank Maureen Riedel and Betsy English at Syracuse University for their help. I could not have done any of the research for this project if it were not for the help of Ed Galvin, Mary O'Brien, and the rest of the staff in the archives department at Syracuse University's Bird Library.

I would also like to thank Sue Edson and Pete Moore, who let me pour through the filing cabinets in the sports information department; Brian Gunning and Kerrin Perniciaro, who assisted a computer illiterate author through the process; and Marlene Ouderkirk, who tolerated my presence in the sports information office for hours on end.

All photographs are provided courtesy of Syracuse University, unless otherwise noted. All rights are reserved.

Finally, I would like to thank my family: my dad for instilling in me my love for sports and writing, my mom for all things other than sports, and my lovely wife Robin and our children, Christopher and Anna Kate, for their encouragement and support during this project.

SYRACUSE'S 1,000TH GAME. On the occasion of Syracuse's 1,000th game, past and present figures gathered. Pictured, from left to right, current Syracuse coach Marc Guley, former coach Lew Andreas, and former coach Edmund Dollard observe Syracuse center Jon Cincebox's shooting form. Dollard, Andreas, and Guley were Syracuse's first three full-time coaches. From 1900 to 1903, the team had no coach. From 1903 to 1911, Syracuse's athletic director John A.R. Scott oversaw the team. Dollard, Andreas, and Guley coached the Orangemen from 1911 to 1962 and combined for a total of 645 victories. In that 1,000th game, on February 15, 1958, Syracuse defeated Colgate University 79-62.

INTRODUCTION

A Tradition of Excellence

Syracuse University fielded its first basketball team in 1900, and ever since the Orangemen have personified excellence on the hardwood. Well, that is not entirely true. In the 1899–1900 academic year, a group of Syracuse University women fielded a basketball team and split a pair of games, beating Cornell University 7-4 and losing to Baron Posse Normal 8-7. The following year, the men's team got started, and thus began a tradition of excellence.

In its 100-plus years, the Syracuse University basketball program has produced 32 different All-Americans. The first was Lewis Castle, a two-time honoree in 1912 and 1914. The most recent was Preston Shumpert (Class of 2002). In between, Syracuse has featured such standout players as Joseph Schwarzer, Vic Hanson, Vince Cohen, Roosevelt Bouie, Louis Orr, Pearl Washington, Derrick Coleman, Sherman Douglas, Billy Owens, Lawrence Moten, John Wallace, and Dave Bing, the greatest player to ever wear orange.

Led by coaches Edmund Dollard, Lew Andreas, Roy Danforth, and Jim Boeheim, the Orangemen have won 3 national titles (including the school's first NCAA championship in 2003), made 29 appearances in the National Collegiate Athletic Association (NCAA) Tournament, and advanced to the Final Four on 4 occasions.

From quaint Archbold Gymnasium to the "Zoo" at Manley Field House to the massive Carrier Dome, Syracuse fans have experienced the best college basketball has to offer. This book uses nearly 190 photographs to look back at the history of Syracuse University basketball, highlighting the players, the coaches, the gyms, the fans, the highs, and the lows. They are all a part of Syracuse's tradition of excellence.

BOUIE RISES FOR A REBOUND. Roosevelt Bouie, a local product from Kendall, New York, was one of Jim Boeheim's first recruits as the head coach at Syracuse. Bouie, a seven-foot-tall center, brought a blend of height, strength, and athleticism. He was an offensive, defensive, and rebounding force. Bouie started all but one game in his career from 1976 to 1980. In those four seasons, he was Syracuse's backbone. He maintained a consistent presence on the boards, averaging between 8.1 and 8.8 rebounds per game in each of his four years at Syracuse. He still ranks 13th in career scoring and 2nd in blocks, behind only Etan Thomas. In 2000, he was named to Syracuse's 25-player All-Century team. (Photograph by Tom Richards.)

One

HOOP ORIGINS
ON THE HILL

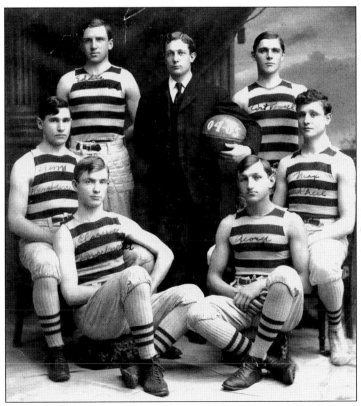

THE 1904–1905 TEAM PHOTOGRAPH. In 1904–1905, the Syracuse Orangemen won 14 games and lost 7. Pictured here, from left to right, are (front row) Clarence Houseknecht and George Redlein; (middle row) George Kirchgasser and Max Rheil; (back row) Edmund Dollard, manager Earl Rice, and captain Arthur Powell.

THE 1902–1903 SYRACUSE SQUAD. Basketball was still in its infancy during the 1902–1903 season. This was just the third recorded year of intercollegiate basketball for Syracuse. The Orangemen won only one game out of nine that season. The team included, from left to right, (front row) C.J. Houseknecht, E.J. Brady, ? Evans, ? Crane, and E.D. Twombley; (middle row) captain Clinton Goodwin, holding the ball; (back row) H.E. Jackman, F.M. Bohr, and Frederick Giffin.

THE "OLD GYM." Prior to the opening of Archbold Gymnasium in 1908, the Orangemen played their games in the "old gym" or the "little red brick band house," which stood on the present site of Hendricks Chapel. Note the old clock as well as the balcony at the top of the photograph.

THE 1903–1904 ORANGEMEN. The Orangemen won 11 games and lost 8 in the 1903–1904 campaign. Identifications of all the men in this photograph could not be made, but the 1904 Onondagan, Syracuse University's student yearbook, lists these as team members: E.K. Twombley, manager F.M. Bohr, C.J. Houseknecht, F.J. Consedine, E.G. Rice, A.J. Brady, H.B. Scott, and C.E. Clinton. The 1903–1904 season marked the first time the university's basketball team had a coach. After three years of abbreviated schedules and no coaching, Syracuse University's athletic director, John A.R. Scott, oversaw the team. He remained in that dual capacity for the next seven seasons.

Syracuse's 1906–1907 Cagers. The 1906–1907 team, which included future Syracuse coach Edmund Dollard, played just seven games against five schools. The Orangemen won four, losing to Colgate twice and Yale once.

Lewis Castle. In 1912, Lewis Castle became Syracuse's first basketball All-American, given that honor by the Helms Foundation. Castle was also named to the 1914 All-American team. From 1912 to 1914, Castle led the Orangemen to a 31-6 record, and the 1913–1914 team went undefeated in 12 games. Castle, who played football as well, is a member of the Helms Foundation Hall of Fame.

THE 1913 ORANGEMEN. In the 1912–1913 season, Edmund Dollard's second season as Syracuse's head coach, the Orangemen won eight games and lost three. All three of Syracuse's losses were on the road while the team remained perfect at home. Dollard suffered his first home loss in his sixth season when the Orange lost to Yale on January 4, 1917. He guided the Orangemen to 151 wins and just 59 losses, a .719 winning percentage, from 1911 to 1924. Dollard played basketball for Syracuse from 1905 to 1908.

THE 1918 HELMS FOUNDATION NATIONAL CHAMPS. Syracuse, coached by Edmund Dollard and led by Joseph Schwarzer, went 16-1 in 1917–1918 and was named national champions by the Helms Foundation of Los Angeles. The team consisted of, from left to right, (front row) John Barsha, John Cronauer, captain Joseph Schwarzer (with the ball), Leon Marcus, and Charles Dolley; (back row) manager H.B. Lowe, Ed Cronauer, coach Edmund Dollard, Russell Finsterwald, manager George Schank, H. Brickman, and trainer Harry Crowley. The

Orangemen won their first 17 games of the season before losing to the University of Pennsylvania 17-16 in the final game of the season. Even though the game was played at Archbold Gym, the Quakers got the better of the officiation, scoring 13 of their 17 points on free throws. Still, the Helms Foundation named Syracuse as its national champions, and Schwarzer earned All-American honors.

THE 1924–1925 ORANGE. The 1924–1925 Syracuse basketball team included, from left to right, the following: (front row) Charles Lee, Vic Hanson, Harlan Carr, captain Henry Greve, Sidney Mendelson, Phillip Rakov, and coach Lew Andreas; (middle row) Lynn Follett, Gordon Mayley, M. Rosser, Albert Ackley, C.R. Fitzsimmons, and Max Boxer; (back row) ? Eck, ? Brodsky, Irving Mendell, Peter Tengi, and manager Robert Semple.

BASKETBALL

1916 -- 17

PRINCETON
vs. SYRACUSE

Archbold Gymnasium   Wed. Eve., Dec. 20

SYRACUSE VERSUS PRINCETON. This game program was sold at the December 20, 1916 game between Syracuse and Princeton. Any fan picking up a copy on the way into Archbold Gym that evening saw a terrific game. Syracuse defeated Princeton 26-25. The Orangemen finished the season with a 13-3 record.

VIC HANSON, ALL-AMERICAN. Though he played almost 80 years ago, Vic Hanson remains one of Syracuse's all-time greats. Hanson was a three-time Helms Foundation All-American from 1925 to 1927. He was the national player of the year in 1927, and he is a member of both the Helms Foundation and Naismith Memorial Halls of Fame. Syracuse compiled a 49-7 record in Hanson's three varsity seasons.

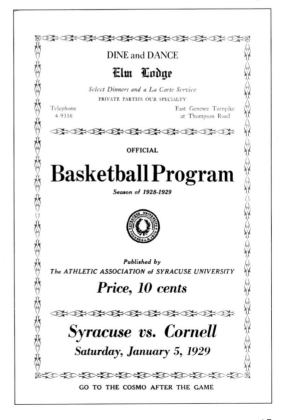

SYRACUSE VERSUS CORNELL. This game program was sold at the 1928–1929 season opener between Syracuse and Cornell at Archbold Gym. The opener was played on January 4, 1929, as Syracuse's first four games that year were cancelled due to a flu epidemic. The Orangemen beat their Ivy League rivals 31-19.

THE 1925–1926 NATIONAL CHAMPIONS. The 1925–1926 Orangemen won 19 games and lost just 1 to earn the Helms Foundation's nod as the national champions. Syracuse was led by coach Lew Andreas, shown here in the middle of the back row, and All-American Vic Hanson, seated in the middle of the first row with the ball. The Orangemen won their first 15 games of the season. In a 30-25 overtime win over the University of Pennsylvania on December 29, Hanson tallied 25 points in perhaps the best game of his career. Syracuse's only loss that season was a 37-31 setback at Penn State when starter Gotch Carr was declared ineligible and Andreas missed the game due to tonsillitis. The Orangemen avenged their only defeat two weeks later, drubbing Penn State 29-12 at home in the next-to-last game of the season.

VIC HANSON, FOOTBALL PLAYER.
Vic Hanson is the only player
inducted in both the College
Football Hall of Fame and the
Naismith Memorial Basketball
Hall of Fame. In 1999, Hanson
was 1 of 44 players named to
Syracuse University's All-Century
football team. He is also a member
of the 25-player All-Century
basketball team. Hanson played
both defensive line and offensive
end for the Orangemen.

VIC HANSON, BASEBALL PLAYER. Vic Hanson was a local
product. He played at Syracuse's Central High and also at
St. John's Manlius. He excelled in several sports, including
basketball and football, but it was reported during
Hanson's collegiate days that baseball was his favorite
sport. Here Hanson, who received a tryout from the
New York Yankees, is shown in his Syracuse University
baseball uniform.

19

THE "REINDEER." The 1929–1930 Syracuse squad was dubbed the "Reindeer" because the five starters were exceedingly fleet of foot. The starting five included, from left to right, captain Louis "Tuppy" Hayman, Daniel Fogarty, Alton Elliott, Kenneth Beagle, and Everett Katz. All were juniors, except Elliott who was a sophomore. Katz developed a one-handed shot several years ahead of Stanford's Hank Luisetti, who is generally credited with the one-hander. Elliott, or "Slim," stood six feet three inches tall and towered over his teammates. The Reindeer won 18 games and lost just 2, at Creighton and Columbia Universities. The Orangemen even defeated the University of Pittsburgh team, which went on to become the national champions with a 23-2 record. The following year, the same Reindeer 5 forged a 16-4 record.

Two
THE ANDREAS ERA

THE 1938–1939 ORANGE. The 1938–1939 Syracuse basketball team posed for this picture. The team consisted of, from left to right, the following: (front row) John Schroeder, Casimer Konstanty, Wilmeth Sidat-Singh, captain Robert Stewart, William Thompson, Abraham Marcus, and Mark Haller; (middle row) Don MacNaughton, Don Werner, Paul Kartluke, William Bolton, John McMillen, Dick Jensen, and Robert Twiford; (back row) Christian Kouray, H. Piro, H. Fitzgerald, D. Avery, J. Rigan, and P. Podbielski.

WILMETH SIDAT-SINGH. In 1937, the legendary Wilmeth Sidat-Singh played on the Syracuse University freshman team. Sidat-Singh, shown here on the far left, played both football and basketball at Syracuse. He was the university's first prominent black athlete. Sidat-Singh, who played briefly with the famous Harlem Rens after college, died on a training flight over the Great Lakes in 1943.

ROBERT TWIFORD. Robert Twiford was a sophomore on the 1938–1939 squad. The Orangemen maintained a steady level of success in those years before World War II under coach Lew Andreas. Syracuse fashioned a 15-4 record in 1939. That was Syracuse's 15th consecutive winning season. The Orangemen extended the streak to 18 seasons before finishing with an 8-10 record in 1942–1943 and then canceling the following season due to the war.

DON SAYLE, CAPTAIN. In the 1941–1942 season, Don Sayle captained the Orangemen. Sayle played at Syracuse from 1940 to 1942. The Orangemen won 15 games and lost just 6 in 1942. At one point, Syracuse won 7 consecutive games before the losses to Penn State and Niagara University in the last 4 games put a damper on the season. This was the 18th consecutive winning season for coach Lew Andreas.

ANDY MOGISH, PLAYER AND COACH. Andy Mogish played basketball at Syracuse in 1943, missed the next three years due to World War II, and then returned to play the 1946–1947 and 1947–1948 seasons. After his playing career, Mogish spent several years as an assistant coach. In particular, Mogish coached Syracuse's freshmen team.

THE 1946 GAME PROGRAM. One of the finest yet relatively unrecognized Orange teams was the 1945–1946 squad. The Orangemen won 23 games that season, more than any Syracuse squad until the 1972–1973 team won 24. Syracuse went 23-2 in the regular season, earning a trip to the National Invitation Tournament (NIT), the school's first postseason appearance. The Orangemen lost to Muhlenberg College 47-41 at Madison Square Garden.

LEW ANDREAS AND ROY PETERS. Syracuse coach Lew Andreas poses with Roy Peters, the captain of the 1946–1947 team. Peters served in World War II and parachuted into France on D-day. He also spent time in a German prison camp. Peters was one of several veterans who played for Syracuse following the war. Billy Gabor, the 1946–1947 squad's leading scorer, was a bombardier, and Larry Crandall flew 35 missions over Italy. Peters only played two years for Syracuse—the 1945–1946 and 1946–1947 seasons. In Peters's senior year, the Orangemen put together a 19-6 record. Syracuse faced the City College of New York (CCNY) in the NCAA District II play-offs at the Troy Armory but lost 61-59.

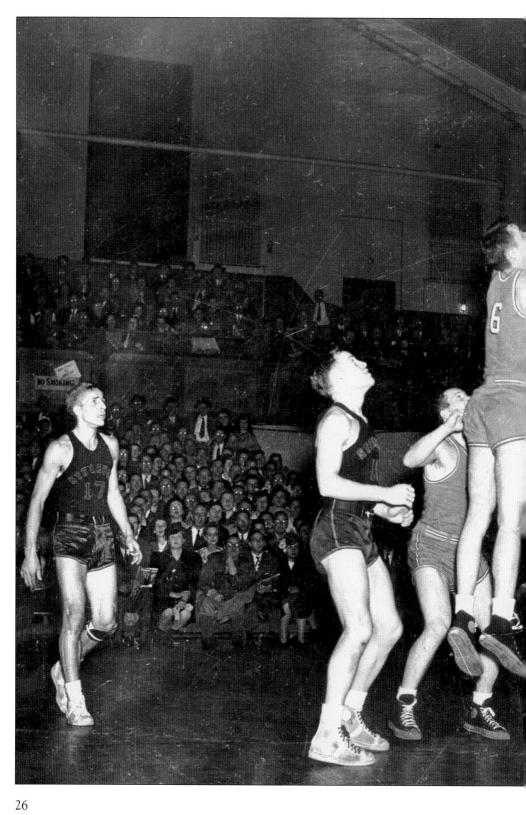

Royce Newell Goes for a Basket. In 1946–1947, the Orangemen were led by three principal players, from left to right, Billy Gabor (No. 17), captain Roy Peters, and Royce Newell (No. 16) shown here attempting a shot. The Orangemen fashioned a 19-6 record despite a January fire at Archbold Gym that left them without a home. Syracuse's season ended with a 61-59 loss to CCNY in the NCAA District II play-offs.

27

FASH DRIVES AGAINST COLGATE. When Syracuse played Colgate in the 1948 season, William Fash drove to the basket as Hank Schulz (No. 31) cleared the way. Colgate was led by All-American Ernie Vandeweghe.

SYRACUSE
VS.
BRIGHAM YOUNG

Dec. 5, 1947

State Fair Coliseum
15c

SYRACUSE VERSUS BRIGHAM YOUNG UNIVERSITY PROGRAM. When the Orangemen faced Brigham Young University (BYU) in the 1947–1948 season, the game took place at the State Fair Coliseum. This was the season-opener for Syracuse, which humbled BYU 74-52. Billy Gabor led the Orangemen that night with 22 points.

BILLY "BULLET" GABOR. From 1946 to 1948, Billy "Bullet" Gabor spearheaded Syracuse's offense. Gabor led the Orangemen in scoring all three years. He also played in 1942–1943 before entering the military during World War II. He totaled 1,344 points for his entire career, making him Syracuse's all-time leading scorer upon graduation. He remained number one on the list until Dave Bing came along in the mid-1960s.

HLADIK SHOOTS AT THE FAIRGROUNDS. The Syracuse Orangemen played most of their home games at the State Fair Coliseum in the 1949–1950 season. In this photograph, Anthony Hladik (No. 34) attempts a shot in a game against Rutgers University while teammates Robert Savage (No. 44) and Earl Ackley (No. 21) look on. The Orangemen managed an 18-9 record that year, which was the final season in Lew Andreas's 25-year coaching career.

ORANGEMEN RETURN TO ARCHBOLD GYM. In January 1947, a fire destroyed Archbold Gym. The Orangemen were without a permanent home for more than a year. In the fall of 1948, Archbold reopened. In this picture, Syracuse coach Lew Andreas makes the first basket at the restored facility. The Orangemen practiced at Archbold but continued to play most of their home games at the State Fair Coliseum, as well as the armory on West Jefferson Street in what is now known as Armory Square. At least, the Orangemen had a place to practice on campus.

31

LEW ANDREAS'S FINAL SQUAD. The 1949–1950 Syracuse Orangemen were Lew Andreas's last team. Andreas, shown here in the middle of the second row, coached the Orangemen for 25 seasons from 1924–1925 through 1950. Andreas's teams won 358 games and lost just 135 for a .726 winning percentage. He suffered just three losing seasons, including two on either side of the 1943–1944 campaign when the university suspended basketball.

Three

GULEY, COHEN, AND AN NCAA BERTH

THE 1950–1951 STARTING FIVE. The highly successful 1950–1951 Syracuse squad boasted the starting lineup of, from left to right, captain Jack Kiley, Dick Suprunowicz, Tom Huggins, Tom Jockle, and Ed Miller. Kiley led the team with 14.4 points per game. Huggins and Miller provided muscle close to the basket. Jockle and Kiley were the ball-handlers. Syracuse went 19-9, wrapping up the season with a win over Bradley University in the National Campus Tournament.

JACK KILEY. For three consecutive seasons, Jack Kiley led Syracuse in scoring. Following in the footsteps of Billy Gabor, Kiley averaged 15.1 points in his career, which included the 1948–1949, 1949–1950, and 1950–1951 seasons. He was the first Syracuse player to score more than 400 points in a season twice.

NATIONAL CAMPUS TOURNAMENT. In 1950–1951, Marc Guley, in his first campaign as Syracuse's head coach, guided the Orangemen to a 19-9 record and the first National Campus Tournament. The tournament was hosted by tournament favorite Bradley University. Syracuse defeated the University of Toledo 69-52 in the first round and then advanced to the finals with a 74-57 win over the University of Utah. In the championship game, the Orangemen stunned Bradley and rallied from an early 24-3 deficit to win 76-75.

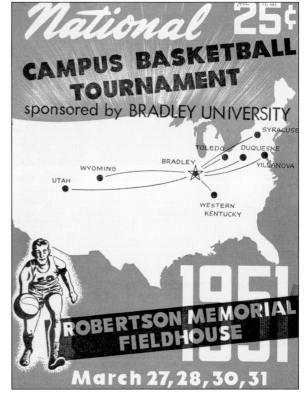

THE 1951–1952 SYRACUSE UNIVERSITY CAGERS. The Orangemen were in their second year under coach Marc Guley in 1951–1952. The team compiled a 14-6 record that year. The team included, from left to right, (front row) William Manikas, Stanley Swanson, Frank Reddout, co-captain Tom Huggins, co-captain Ed Miller, Robert Roche, Melvin Besdin, and Peter Stark; (back row) assistant coach Andy Mogish, ? Reuhel, manager Stanley Rose, Charles Thaw, Jack Larned, David Kline, ? Eischen, Daniel Jackimaiak, ? Large, and coach Marc Guley.

ED MILLER. Ed Miller, the co-captain of Syracuse's 1951–1952 squad, led the Orangemen against Brigham Young University in the home-opener on December 10. The Orangemen won 63-58. In the season-opener at Canisius College nine days earlier, Miller scored 40 points in a 92-76 victory. Only three Syracuse players have ever scored more in a single game: Dave Bing (three times), Bill Smith (two times), and Pete Chudy (once).

REDDOUT'S REBOUNDS. Frank Reddout holds one of the longest-standing records in Syracuse history. Reddout, who played at Syracuse from 1951 to 1953, pulled down 34 rebounds against Temple University on February 9, 1952. No Orangeman has ever come close to Reddout's mark. Dave Bing's 25 rebounds against Cornell University on February 8, 1966, compile the next-highest total in the university history.

THE 1953 ORANGEMEN. In this undated photograph, Syracuse standout Frank Reddout is pictured in the back row fourth from the right. Reddout lettered in 1951, 1952, and 1953. This is believed to be the 1952–1953 team, which struggled to a 7-11 record. Reddout led the team in scoring with 16.8 points per game.

THE 1953–1954 ORANGEMEN. The starting five on the 1953–1954 Syracuse squad consisted of, from left to right, Jack Larned, Dick Jaskot, Mel Besdin, Dave Kline, and Ronnie Kilpatrick. Besdin led the Orangemen in scoring and averaged 16.1 points per game. The Orangemen put together a 10-9 record that season, highlighted by a sweep of Colgate.

THE VETERANS OF THE 1954–1955 SQUAD. In the 1954–1955 season, the Orangemen struggled to a 10-11 record. The team's upperclassmen included, from left to right, (front row) Jack Larned, Charles Thaw, Louis Cegala, and August Castellini; (back row) Ronald Gillespie, Manny Breland, and "Moose" Murdock.

THE 1955–1956 ORANGE. Syracuse rebounded from three straight mediocre campaigns with a 14-8 record in 1955–1956. The Orangemen were, from left to right, (front row) Vince Cohen, Louis Cegala, Jack Larned, Vincent Albanese, Lewis Stark, and coach Marc Guley; (back row) assistant coach Andy Mogish, Ronald Gillespie, August Castellini, Gary Clark, ? Roper, James Snyder, Manny Breland, Jim Brown, and assistant coach ? Reuhel.

SYRACUSE'S 200-PLUS QUINTET. In the 1955–1956 season, Syracuse had five players who scored at least 200 points apiece. The Orangemen played just 22 games that season. Shown, from left to right, are Jim Brown, James Snyder, Gary Clark, Vince Cohen, and team captain Ronald Gillespie. Cohen was the team's high scorer with 401 points for an average of 18.2 points per game.

JIM BROWN IN ACTION. In a rare action photograph, Jim Brown, who starred in both football and lacrosse and also played a little basketball while at Syracuse University, makes a basket against Canisius College during the 1954–1955 season. Brown played basketball for the Orangemen in 1954–1955 as well as the 1955–1956 season and was a double-figure scorer. Former Syracuse lacrosse coach Roy Simmons Jr. has called Brown one of the best lacrosse players he has ever seen. However, Brown is best known for his exploits on the football field. An All-American running back, Brown went on to have a brilliant career with the National Football League's (NFL) Cleveland Browns. He is a member of the college and professional football halls of fame. Also pictured here is Vince Cohen, No. 34, a Helms Foundation All-American in 1957.

SYRACUSE'S FIRST NCAA TOURNAMENT TEAM. In 1956–1957, the Syracuse Orangemen earned the first NCAA Tournament bid in school history. That year's team included, from left to right, (front row) Ron McCane, Ted Parke, Vince Cohen, Larry Loudis, Vince Albanese, Wayne Leach, Bill Houghton, and Bruce Schmelzer; (back row) freshmen coach Andy Mogish, Manny Breland, Hal Noyes, Gary Clark, Jim Snyder, Gary Evans, Jon Cincebox, Dave Hollenbeck, Maury Youmans, George Crofoot, and coach Marc Guley. The Orangemen defeated the University of Connecticut and Lafayette College in the tournament before losing to North Carolina 67-58.

THE VETERANS OF THE 1957 NCAA SQUAD. The 1956–1957 Orangemen, Syracuse's first NCAA Tournament team, won 16 regular season games against just 6 losses and finished with an 18-7 record. The team's veterans are shown here, from left to right, as follows: (front row) Vincent Albanese and Vince Cohen; (back row) Larry Loudis, Manny Breland, Jon Cincebox, coach Marc Guley, Gary Clark, and Harold Noyes.

AN OUTSTANDING REBOUNDER, JON CINCEBOX. Jon Cincebox, who played at Syracuse from 1957 to 1959, is one of the greatest rebounders in Syracuse history. Cincebox, who stood six feet seven inches tall and weighed 225 pounds, completed his career with 1,004 rebounds. That total remains the fourth-highest total in Syracuse history—behind Derrick Coleman, Rony Seikaly, and John Wallace—and the highest of any three-year player.

VINCE COHEN. The 1956–1957 Orangemen were led by senior Vince Cohen. Cohen, shown here in a game against Columbia, averaged 24.2 points per game that season. Since Syracuse started keeping official scoring records in 1946, only 2 players have averaged more in a single season than Cohen's 24.2 mark: Dave Bing with 28.4 in 1966 and Greg Kohls with 26.7 in 1972. It was the third straight season Cohen was Syracuse's leading scorer. He finished his three-year varsity career with 1,337 points, which still ranks 28th on Syracuse's all-time list. At the end of the 1956–1957 season, the Helms Foundation named Cohen to its 30-player All-American team.

SYRACUSE'S 1958–1959 CAGERS. A strong finish enabled the Orangemen to a 14-9 record in the 1958–1959 season. Syracuse won its last seven games to salvage the campaign. Pictured, from left to right, are the following: Ed Goldberg, Sanford Salz, Bruce Schmelzer, John Mustion, Steve Berkenfeld, Tom Mossey, Bruce Kollath, Pete Chudy, Harold Noyes, Jon Cincebox, Doug Yarnall, trainer ? Reichel, head coach Marc Guley, and assistant coach Andy Mogish.

THE SYRACUSE QUINTET. Five Syracuse players posed for this undated picture sometime between 1956 and 1958. Pictured, from left to right, are Gary Evans, Dave Hollenbeck, Stan Watson, Ron McCane, and Larry Loudis. All but Watson were members of the 1957 NCAA Tournament team. It may be that these were Syracuse's five scholarship freshmen in 1955.

DICK FINLEY, LACROSSE ALL-AMERICAN. Dick Finley played both basketball and lacrosse at Syracuse in the early 1960s. Finley combined both sports in this photograph. He experienced more success on the lacrosse field than the basketball court. A standout midfielder, Finley was an honorable mention All-America in 1960, a third-team honoree in 1961, and a first-team All-America in 1962.

DOUG YARNALL. Doug Yarnall, a six-foot-eight-inch center from West Chester, Pennsylvania, played at Syracuse in the early 1960s. The Orangemen struggled in the early part of that decade. After going to the 1957 NCAA Tournament, Syracuse's successes steadily declined with win totals of 11, 14, 13, 4, and 2 over the next five seasons.

FROM DIAMOND TO HARDWOOD. Dave Giusti, right, and John Mustion, left, played both baseball and basketball at Syracuse. The two were freshmen in 1959. Giusti, who never lettered in basketball according to the school's media guide, played shortstop and pitcher at the university. Mustion pitched and also played outfield. Giusti had a long Major League baseball career as a pitcher and spent most of his career with the Pittsburgh Pirates.

GRAB AN OAR. This Orangeman would look at lot more familiar with an oar in his hands instead of a basketball. Bill Sanford, a six-foot-seven-inch-tall forward, played a little basketball at Syracuse in the early 1960s, but he practically personifies Syracuse's rowing program. Sanford captained the 1963 rowing team. In 1968, he became the university's rowing coach. Sanford has tutored five Olympic rowers.

45

THE DOWN YEARS. The early 1960s marked one of the lowest periods in Syracuse basketball history. Syracuse still boasted several quality players, such as Pete Chudy, Fred Machemer, Mannie Klutschkowski, and Herb Foster, but the overall results were not the same as in the mid-1950s. Here, Syracuse coach Marc Guley poses with Fred Machemer, the captain of the 1961–1962 team. That year, which was the last of Guley's 12-year career, the Orangemen finished with a 2-22 record, coming on the heels of a 4-19 record the previous year. Syracuse had not experienced a worse season since the 1902–1903 squad went 1-8, beating only Potsdam Normal. But things were about to change on the Syracuse University Hill.

Four

MANLEY FIELD HOUSE AND DAVE BING

THE MANLEY FIELD HOUSE ERA. The Syracuse Orangemen moved into Manley Field House at the start of the 1962–1963 season and stayed there until 1980. In the first game at Manley, Syracuse defeated Kent State 36-35 on December 1, 1962. The Orangemen won 190 games at Manley and lost just 28. Syracuse also posted home-win streaks of 36 and 57 games at Manley.

DAVE BING, ALL-AMERICAN. Dave Bing is one of the most decorated players in Syracuse basketball history. Bing earned All-American honors in both 1965 and 1966. He was the National Basketball Association's (NBA) Rookie of the Year in 1967 and was voted one of the 50 greatest players in NBA history. Both Syracuse University and the Detroit Pistons have retired his number. He is a member of the Naismith Memorial Basketball Hall of Fame.

SOPHOMORE BING GRACES THE MEDIA GUIDE COVER. The Syracuse University sports information department made no bones when it put Dave Bing, a sophomore, on the cover of the 1963–1964 media guide. The guide, which was the size of a pamphlet, noted that Bing had led Syracuse's freshman team in scoring, rebounding, and assists the previous year.

SYRACUSE UNIVERSITY BASKETBALL

1963-64 63rd Season

FRED LEWIS WITH CO-CAPTAINS. The 1964–1965 campaign marked Fred Lewis's third season as head coach of the Orangemen. Here, Lewis poses with the 1964–1965 team co-captains Chuck Richards (left) and Dave Bing (right). Bing led the Orangemen in scoring and rebounding with 23.2 points and 12 rebounds per game. Syracuse won 11 of its last 13 games to finish with a 13-10 record and signal what would be a terrific 1965–1966 season.

LEWIS AND RICHARDS. In addition to Dave Bing, another new arrival helped to turn Syracuse's basketball program around in the 1960s. Chuck Richards, a six-foot-eight-inch tall transfer from West Point Academy, gave Syracuse a strong inside presence in the 1963–1964 and 1964–1965 seasons. Richards averaged 9.1 rebounds per game in 1964.

49

JIM BOEHEIM, THE PLAYER. Jim Boeheim came to Syracuse in 1962 from nearby Lyons, where he earned all-state honors at Lyons Central High School. An invited walk-on, Boeheim quickly proved he could play. He became a co-captain with the legendary Dave Bing on the 1965–1966 team. As a senior, Boeheim averaged 14.6 points per game. In 1969, he embarked on another career, joining Roy Danforth's coaching staff as a graduate assistant.

CARL VERNICK. Carl Vernick spanned two eras in Syracuse basketball history. As a sophomore, Vernick played on the 1962–1963 squad that finished with a 2-22 record. Two years later, Vernick was a senior on the 1963–1964 team, which went 17-8. Vernick, a six-foot-tall guard from Philadelphia, led the Orangemen in scoring as a sophomore and as a junior.

THE MANLEY "ZOO." Syracuse fans are as much a part of Syracuse basketball as the players and coaches themselves. Known today for setting NCAA attendance records at the Carrier Dome, Syracuse fans during the Manley Field House era were known for their raucous behavior. They turned Manley into a snake pit for opposing teams. The noise at Manley would echo off the roof and seemingly magnify as it bounced around the arena. Dust from the old dirt floor would rise up during games. Thus, the rowdy student section became known as the "Zoo." Manley was the only home Syracuse stars such as Dave Bing, Vaughn Harper, Bill Smith, Greg Kohls, Rudy Hackett, Roosevelt Bouie, and Louis Orr ever knew. The atmosphere helped the Orangemen win 87.1 percent of their games at Manley from its opening in 1962 to its close in 1980.

THE 1965–1966 SYRACUSE ORANGEMEN. The 1966 Orangemen made the school's second trip to the NCAA Tournament, following up on the 1957 team's appearance. The team was led by seniors Dave Bing and Jim Boeheim, and Fred Lewis was in his fourth season as the team's head coach. The Orangemen went 22-6 in 1966. Syracuse defeated Davidson College in the East Region semifinals before losing to Duke University in the next round. The team consisted

of these men, from left to right: (front row) manager Bernie Fine; (back row) head coach Fred
Lewis, Rex Trobridge, Vaughn Harper, Norm Goldsmith, George Hicker, Sam Penceal, Steve
Ludd, Tom Bednark, Richie Cornwall, Frank Nicoletti, Tom Ringelmann, Jim Boeheim, Dave
Bing, Dick Ableman, Rick Dean, Val Reid, and freshman coach Roy Danforth.

DAVE BING. Dave Bing brought an exciting style to Syracuse basketball. He and his fellow freshmen regularly beat the 1962–1963 varsity squad. The stories have been told often of fans watching the freshmen play and then leaving prior to the varsity game. In addition, several near-capacity crowds would come to watch the freshmen even when there was no varsity contest to follow. In Bing's sophomore year, his first as a varsity player, the Orangemen posted a 17-8 record, just two years after a 2-22 season. Bing, pictured here soaring to the basket against Cornell with Jim Boeheim (No. 35, at right) looking on, scored 1,883 points in his three varsity seasons. He averaged 28.4 points per game as a senior. Syracuse has had just 10, 40-plus point games, and Bing is responsible for 4 of those. Bing was a stellar rebounder as well as a scorer. He averaged double figures in both scoring and rebounding as both a junior and a senior.

SYRACUSE RETIRES NO. 22. In 1981, Syracuse University retired Dave Bing's No. 22. The only other basketball numbers that Syracuse has retired are Vic Hanson's No. 8 and Dwayne "Pearl" Washington's No. 31. All three numbers hang from the blue curtain behind the bleachers at Syracuse's games. The last Orangeman to actually wear No. 22 was Eddie Moss.

DAVE BING ENTERS THE HALL OF FAME. On May 15, 1990, Dave Bing was inducted into the Naismith Memorial Basketball Hall of Fame in Springfield, Massachusetts. Bing, at left, is pictured with fellow inductees Elvin Hayes and Earl Monroe. Bing joined Vic Hanson as the only Syracuse Orangemen in the basketball hall of fame.

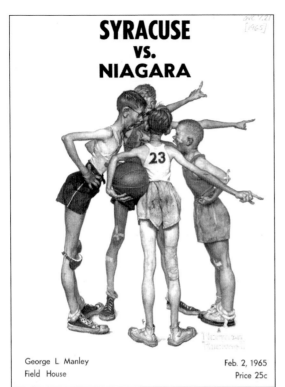

SYRACUSE
VS.
NIAGARA

23

George L. Manley
Field House

Feb. 2, 1965
Price 25c

THE NORMAN ROCKWELL PROGRAM COVER. The cover of a game program from a February 2, 1965 contest that pitted Syracuse against visiting Niagara University featured a Norman Rockwell illustration of four boys in a heated argument. The Orangemen handed Niagara an 83-76 loss that night. (Photograph by Lennox "Red" McLendon.)

VAL REID. Val Reid, whose full name was Valentine Reid, played for Syracuse in 1965 and 1966. Reid played a valuable role as a reserve on the 1966 NCAA Tournament team, a squad that boasted talent all the way down to the 12th man. (Photograph by Robert Lorenz.)

56

SAM PENCEAL. The 1965–1966 team was noted for seniors Dave Bing and Jim Boeheim and sophomores George Hicker and Vaughn Harper, but the Orangemen relied on a cohesive mix of talent, including senior Sam Penceal. Penceal contributed in many ways, but he was noted for his defensive ability.

FRANK NICOLETTI. Another member of the Class of 1966, Frank Nicoletti played a reserve role during the Bing era. Nicoletti, a top player from New Jersey, provided defense and hustle off the bench for the Orangemen. (Photograph by Lennox "Red" McLendon.)

THE 1966–1967 STARTING FIVE. The starting five from the 1966–1967 squad huddle up prior to a game. In the middle is starting point guard Richie Cornwall. The rest of the starting five consisted of George Hicker, Rick Dean, Vaughn Harper, and Steve Ludd. At one point in the 1967 campaign, the Orangemen were 19-2 and ranked eighth in the nation before losing four of their last five games.

THE HICKER FLICKER. Dave Bing led Syracuse in scoring from 1964 to 1966. In 1966–1967, the Orangemen's leading scorer was George Hicker, who averaged 18.6 points per game. Hicker is shown here cutting to the basket, but he scored most of his points on a soft outside jump shot that became known as the "Hicker Flicker."

VAUGHN HARPER. Vaughn Harper was a three-year starter from 1966 to 1968 for the Orangemen. As a sophomore, Vaughn started all but three games for Syracuse's NCAA East Region finalists. As a senior, he led the Orangemen in scoring. Vaughn, pictured here going after a rebound against LaSalle University in 1968, still ranks 10th on Syracuse's all-time rebounding chart despite playing just three varsity campaigns.

A GAME PROGRAM FROM THE 1967–1968 SEASON. In the late 1960s, game programs took on a cartoonish nature. The December 15, 1967 game between Syracuse and Penn State featured this program cover. The Orangemen won 90-89 in overtime.

CORNWALL GOES AIRBORNE. A dynamic floor leader, Richie Cornwall attempts a falling down shot against the College of the Holy Cross in the 1966–1967 season. In the year after Dave Bing's final season at Syracuse, the Orangemen relied on the likes of Cornwall, George Hicker, Rick Dean, and Vaughn Harper to fashion a 20-6 record. The Orangemen earned an invitation to the NIT where they suffered a 66-64 first-round loss to the University of New Mexico.

SYRACUSE VERSUS COLGATE. Since Syracuse first fielded a basketball team in 1900, the Orangemen have played Colgate more often than any other opponent. Including the 2001–2002 season, Syracuse and Colgate had met on the hardwood 157 times, and the Orangemen won on 109 occasions. In comparison, Syracuse has played Big East foe Georgetown University just 69 times. Syracuse and Colgate first met in the 1901–1902 season and split a pair of games.

The Saltine Warrior. The Saltine Warrior, shown here on the cover of the 1968–1969 media guide, began as a hoax. In a 1931 edition of the Syracuse Orange Peel, it was reported that the remains of a 16th-century Onondagan chief were discovered in the excavation of the women's gymnasium. It was not until 1951 that the Saltine Warrior (a member of the Lambda Chi Alpha fraternity dressed in a costume) made his first appearance at a university football game. Syracuse University officials retired the Saltine Warrior in 1978 when members of a Native American student organization protested the characterization of Native Americans.

SYRACUSE
UNIVERSITY
BASKETBALL

1968-69

Compliments of Varsity Club

The Long and the Short of the Orange. In the 1968–1969 season, Tom Green (left) and Bill Smith (right) summed up the small and the tall of Syracuse hoops. Green stood just 5 feet 11 inches tall. Smith was a foot taller. Though just a sophomore, Smith led the Orangemen in both scoring and rebounding with 19 points and 11.6 rebounds per game.

GREG "KID" KOHLS. In the 1971–1972 season, Greg "Kid" Kohls put together one of the most prolific years in Syracuse history. Kohls, shown here in a game against Fordham University on February 9, 1972, scored 748 points that year. His 26.7 scoring average is the second highest in recorded history at Syracuse, trailing only Dave Bing's 28.4 mark in 1965–1966.

MARK WADACH. As the Syracuse basketball program began to pick up steam in the early 1970s, it was players like Mark Wadach who led the way. The Orangemen had been absent from postseason play for three years when they earned an NIT berth in 1970–1971. They went back to the NIT the next year and then received the first of eight consecutive NCAA bids in 1972–1973. Wadach, shown here in a 1972–1973 game against LaSalle, started every game in those three seasons.

DuVal Shoots Down the Jaspers. In the early 1970s, Dennis DuVal put together two special back-to-back offensive seasons. In 1972–1973, as a junior, DuVal, pictured here in a game against Manhattan College, averaged 19.5 points per game. The next year, DuVal averaged 22.2 points per game. Since then, only one Syracuse player has averaged more in a season—Billy Owens.

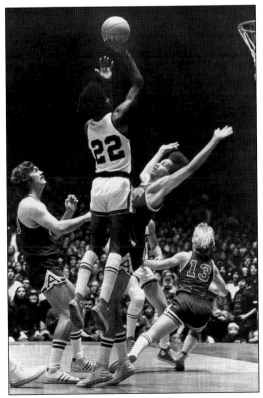

Dennis DuVal. Dennis DuVal was Syracuse's leading scorer in both the 1972–1973 and 1973–1974 seasons. DuVal, shown here taking a shot in a game against American University in the 1972–1973 season, scored 1,504 points in just three years of varsity competition. He remains Syracuse's 16th all-time scorer, 3rd among players with only three years of varsity basketball.

Two of Smith's Record 47. On January 14, 1971, Syracuse senior center Bill Smith torched visiting Lafayette for 47 points. That figure still stands as the Syracuse record for most points scored in a single game. In this photograph, Smith scores 2 of his record 47 points. Smith's 47 points eclipsed Dave Bing's record of 46 points, which he set on December 28, 1965, against Vanderbilt University in the Los Angeles Classic. Smith led Syracuse in scoring in 1971 with a 22.7 point-per-game average. Smith also led the Orange in the 1968–1969 season, averaging 19.0 points per game as a sophomore. It was that season, in just his second varsity game, that Smith scored 41 points in a 118-110 loss to Niagara University on December 7, 1968. Niagara's Calvin Murphy scored 68 points for the Purple Eagles, which remains the most ever scored by a single player against Syracuse.

Five

A BANNER ERA UNFOLDS

A BEVY OF BANNERS. The 1970s marked a highly successful era for Syracuse University basketball. The Orangemen raised several banners to the Manley Field House rafters, marking their achievements. The Orangemen went to the NIT in 1971, beginning a streak of postseason appearances that continued until the 1992–1993 season. Syracuse advanced to its first Final Four in 1975. Prior to 1971, Syracuse had made four appearances in the NIT and just two in the NCAA Tournament. (Photograph by Lawrence Mason Jr.)

THE 1974–1975 TEAM CAPTAINS. Rudy Hackett (left) and Jim Lee (right) captained the 1974–1975 Syracuse team that made it to the NCAA Tournament's Final Four. Hackett led the team in scoring and rebounding while Lee led in assists. Both Hackett and Lee earned All-American honors and were later named to Syracuse University's All-Century team.

ROY DANFORTH. Roy Danforth coached the Orangemen for just eight seasons, starting with the 1968–1969 season and ending with the 1975–1976 campaign, but his tenure was a significant period for Syracuse University hoops. Danforth's first team earned a 9-16 record, but the Orangemen won 139 games and lost just 55 over the next seven years. He guided the Orangemen to two NIT berths and four NCAA appearances, including the 1975 Final Four.

JIM LEE. Jim Lee, shown here in a 1974–1975 contest against LaSalle, provided the backcourt leadership on Syracuse's 1975 Final Four squad. Lee led the Orangemen in assists and also contributed perimeter scoring. His .859 career free throw percentage (243 out of 283) ranks second in school history behind Richie Cornwall's .861 mark. (Photograph by Dennis McDonald.)

RUDY HACKETT. In the Final Four season of 1974–1975, senior forward Rudy Hackett led the Syracuse Orangemen with 22.2 points and 12.7 rebounds per game. Shown here in a game against Penn State that year, Hackett remains Syracuse's fifth-ranked career rebounder with 990 despite playing just three varsity seasons.

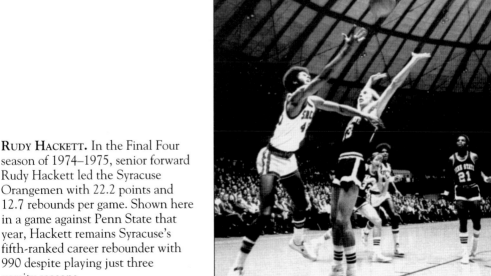

Practice at Archbold in 1974. Prior to the start of the 1974–1975 season, the Orangemen had to practice on a court in Archbold Gym while the floor at Manley Field House was being renovated. For more than 10 years, Manley Field House's floor was made of dirt. The dust would hang in the air during games. In the fall of 1974, though, Manley was outfitted with a new synthetic floor. Several familiar faces can be picked out of this photograph that shows the Orangemen in a basic two-line passing drill. At left, behind the players is assistant Jim Boeheim. In the foreground on the right is Jim Williams. On the far end of the line of players on the right is team co-captain Rudy Hackett. The Orangemen moved back into Manley in time to embark on a ride that would not end until the Final Four in San Diego. (Photograph by Dennis McDonald.)

PROVIDENCE IS DIVINE. The Syracuse Orangemen stunned the University of North Carolina in the 1975 East Region semifinals in Providence, 78-76, to move within a game of the Final Four. Jim Lee, shown here inbounding the ball against the defensive pressure of North Carolina's Phil Ford, hit the game-winning basket with five seconds remaining. (Photograph by Thomas F. Maguire Jr.)

THE 1975 FINAL FOUR PROGRAM. The cover of the 1975 Final Four program featured an action shot from the previous year's Final Four. North Carolina State's David Thompson soars toward the basket over UCLA's Bill Walton. Walton and the Bruins were back in the 1975 Final Four along with the University of Kentucky, the University of Louisville, and eastern underdog Syracuse.

THE ORANGEMEN TAKE ON KENTUCKY. In their first appearance in the NCAA Tournament's Final Four, the Syracuse Orangemen challenged the No. 2-ranked Kentucky Wildcats. The Orangemen advanced to the Final Four with tournament wins over LaSalle, North Carolina, and Kansas State. Kentucky beat back upstart Syracuse 95-79 in San Diego's Sports Arena. In this photograph, Syracuse's Jim Williams attempts a shot against Kentucky. He was one of the heroes in the Orangemen's overtime win over Kansas State with his last-second dash up-court and pass to Rudy Hackett for a basket that sent the game into overtime. Williams injured his right shoulder in the semifinal contest against Kentucky but played through the injury. (Photograph by Tom Killips.)

HACKETT IN THE FINAL FOUR. Syracuse senior co-captain Rudy Hackett tries to stop Kentucky center Bob Guyette in the 1975 semifinals. Hackett scored 14 points but wound up with just 5 rebounds. Hackett found himself in foul trouble for much of the game and played a mere 28 minutes. His foul problems played a big role in the game's outcome, as the Wildcats out-rebounded the Orangemen 57 to 40. (Photograph by Tom Killips.)

CHRIS SEASE. In the 1975 NCAA semifinals against Kentucky, Syracuse junior Chris Sease put together a standout game. Sease scored 18 points and contributed 10 rebounds. His performance was not enough to stop the Wildcats, who handed the Orangemen a 95-79 loss. (Photograph by Tom Killips.)

71

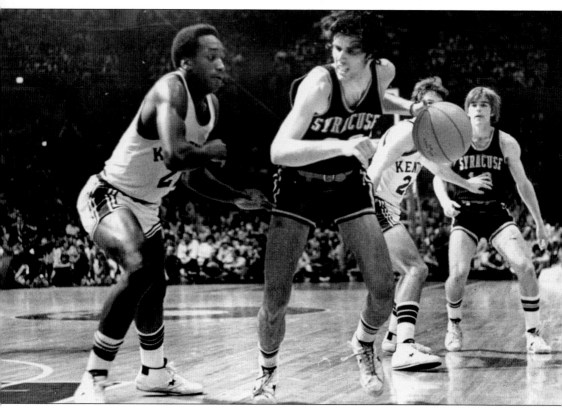

KEVIN KING LOOKS TO SCORE. Kevin King, shown here with the ball, tries to find a way around Kentucky's Jack Givens in the 1975 NCAA semifinals. The Orangemen connected on 49 percent of their field goal attempts, but the Wildcats used a 57-40 edge on the boards to end Syracuse's dream season. Givens proved to be the man of the night for Kentucky. Only a freshman, Givens scored 24 points to lead all scorers and also contributed 11 rebounds.

THE 1975 NCAA FINAL FOUR SQUAD. Syracuse made its first Final Four appearance in 1975 under coach Roy Danforth. Syracuse was still a regional school. The farthest west the Orangemen traveled was St. Bonaventure and the farthest south was Temple, until the NCAA Tournament. The Orangemen defeated LaSalle, stunned North Carolina, and came back two days later to beat Kansas State in overtime to earn a trip to the Final Four in San Diego. The Orangemen lost to Kentucky in the semifinals and then dropped a consolation game against Louisville, but the 1975 season remains one of the greatest years in Syracuse history. The 1974–1975 squad included these men, from left to right: (front row) assistant coach Tom Green, Larry Arrington, Larry Kelley, head coach Roy Danforth, Ross Kindel, Jim Lee, Jim Williams, and assistant coach Jim Boeheim; (back row) Mark Meadors, Steve Shaw, Kevin King, Chris Sease, Bob Parker, Rudy Hackett, Earnie Seibert, Bruce DeBord, Marty Byrnes, Bill DeMarle, Kevin James, Don Degner, and Mike Danforth.

THE BOEHEIM ERA BEGINS. Jim Boeheim took over the Syracuse head coaching position on April 3, 1976, after Roy Danforth's departure to Tulane University. A hastily assembled search committee considered a handful of candidates, including Rutgers University coach Tom Young and University of Michigan assistant Bill Frieder, before choosing Boeheim. Boeheim, the former Syracuse player and assistant coach, immediately put his stamp on the program. Boeheim's first hire as an assistant coach was Rick Pitino. Boeheim tracked Pitino down in New York on the day after Pitino's wedding. Shortly thereafter, Boeheim brought Bernie Fine, the one-time Syracuse University manager and then Henninger High School coach, on board. The Orangemen won 100 games in Boeheim's first 4 seasons, making him the fastest coach to 100 wins in NCAA Division I history. He guided the Orangemen to the NCAA Tournament in 14 of his first 16 seasons at the helm.

THE 1976–1977 COACHING STAFF.
The 1976–1977 season was Jim Boeheim's first as Syracuse's head coach. Boeheim, shown here kneeling, is pictured with his first coaching staff. Boeheim's assistants, from left to right, are Rick Pitino, Mark Meadors, and Bernie Fine. The Orangemen won 26 games and lost just 4 in Boeheim's first year.

BOEHEIM'S SIDELINE THEATRICS.
Few college coaches have a face as expressive as that of Jim Boeheim. In this photograph, taken during a 1981 game against Old Dominion University, Boeheim angrily reacts to a referee's call. Players, referees, the media, and even the fans have been the subject of a Boeheim rant.

DALE SHACKLEFORD. Dale Shackleford came to Syracuse from nearby Utica in the fall of 1975. Over the next four seasons, he played on four NCAA Tournament teams. He led the Orangemen in rebounding as both a freshman and a sophomore. He still ranks 11th in career rebounds with 851. (Photograph by Joe Wrinn.)

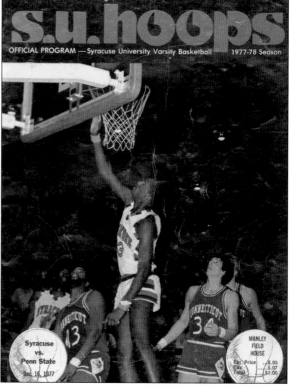

SYRACUSE VERSUS PENN STATE. Dale Shackleford made the cover of the game program when Syracuse played host to Penn State on December 16, 1977, at Manley Field House. Shackleford, a junior, led the Orange in rebounding the two previous years. On this night, Syracuse defeated the Nittany Lions 81-45.

JIM "BUG" WILLIAMS. Jim "Bug" Williams played a significant role in Syracuse basketball history on the court but an even more important one off the court. As a sophomore, Williams was a key member of the 1975 Final Four squad. Williams then led Syracuse in scoring in the 1975–1976 and 1976–1977 seasons. Off the court, Williams led a group of veteran players to go in front of the search committee and endorsed then-assistant Jim Boeheim as the team's choice to succeed Roy Danforth. (Photograph by Bob Sacha.)

MARTY BYRNES. Marty Byrnes was Syracuse's leading scorer in the 1977–1978 season, averaging 16.3 points per game. Byrnes helped the Orangemen to a 22-6 record that season, which ended with an 87-86 overtime loss to Western Kentucky University in the first round of the NCAA Tournament. Byrnes, a member of Syracuse's All-Century team, was a first-round draft choice of the Phoenix Suns in 1978 and played for four years in the NBA.

THE FIRST CARRIER CLASSIC. The first Carrier Classic took place before there was Carrier Dome. Manley Field House hosted the inaugural event on December 2 and 3, 1977. The tournament featured Syracuse, Michigan State University, the University of Rhode Island, and LeMoyne College. The Orangemen captured the championship with a 75-67 victory over Michigan State and Earvin "Magic" Johnson.

ERICH SANTIFER. Erich Santifer played his freshman year at Manley Field House before spending the next three years at the Carrier Dome. In this photograph, Santifer worms his way for two points against Siena College on February 4, 1980, at Manley. Santifer would finish his career with 1,860 points, which still places him ninth among the school's career-scoring leaders.

MARTY HEADD. One of the most recognizable players in Syracuse history, Marty Headd played from 1977 to 1981. Headd, whose bald pate made him stand out instantly, was a deadly perimeter shooter and one of the school's most accurate free throw shooters. After coming off the bench as a freshman, Headd started his sophomore, junior, and senior years on teams that had a combined record of 74-20.

THE LOUIE AND BOUIE SHOW. The Louie and Bouie Show, starring Louis Orr and Roosevelt Bouie, ran at Syracuse University from 1976–1977 to 1979–1980. In the Louie and Bouie era, the Orangemen put together a four-season run, going 26-4, 22-6, 26-4, and 26-4 for a combined record of 100-18. Syracuse went to the NCAA Tournament four straight years. The Louie and Bouie Show coincided with the beginning of the Jim Boeheim coaching era. Bouie, a seven-foot-tall player from nearby Kendall, New York, was Boeheim's first recruit. Boeheim sent new assistant Rick Pitino to Cincinnati to see Orr, a skinny six-foot-nine-inch tall forward. Bouie and Orr personified a shift in college basketball as the "athletic big man" began to change the way the game looked. This picture provides the perfect example as Orr dribbles the ball on the break with Bouie trailing him on the outside. Orr would go on to the NBA where he played with the Indiana Pacers and New York Knicks in an eight-year career. Bouie took his game overseas, enjoying an immensely successful professional career in Italy.

ROOSEVELT BOUIE. Roosevelt Bouie was more than just one-half of the Louie and Bouie Show, he was a dominating player at Syracuse. His career totals included 1,560 points (which ranks 11th in school history), 987 rebounds (6th), and 327 blocks (2nd behind Etan Thomas). Bouie earned All-American honors in both 1979 and 1980. (Photograph by Lawrence Mason Jr.)

LOUIS ORR. Orr, shown here grabbing a rebound as Roosevelt Bouie watches, teamed up with Bouie on a formidable front line at Syracuse. Consider that Orr's career totals were 1,487 points and 881 rebounds while sharing the wealth with his running mate for all four years. Orr never led Syracuse in scoring. He led the Orangemen in rebounding just once, as a senior, and yet he still ranks ninth on the school's all-time list. (Photograph by Lawrence Mason Jr.)

TEAMMATES EVEN AS ALUMNI. Jim Boeheim and Dave Bing played together at Syracuse University from 1962 to 1966 and again in 1979 for an alumni game at Manley Field House. Boeheim and Bing are the two most important figures in Syracuse basketball history. Bing is regarded as the best player in school history. He single-handedly resurrected the sport at Syracuse. When he arrived in 1962, legend has it that some fans would attend the freshmen games at Manley only to leave when the varsity, which had an 8-13 record that year, took the court. Bing led Syracuse in scoring during all three of his varsity years, including a school-record 28.4 points per game in 1966. Boeheim, a non-scholarship player made the most of his abilities as a player and later made his most significant contributions as a coach. He took over for Roy Danforth in 1976–1977 and won 100 games in his first four years. He now has over 600 wins and two Final Four appearances. (Photograph by Glen Stubbe.)

Six

The Carrier Dome Opens

The Carrier Dome Era. The Carrier Dome opened in 1980 and began setting NCAA attendance records soon thereafter. Even coach Jim Boeheim had questioned the wisdom of the move from Manley and whether his Orangemen would enjoy the same home-court advantage. But when crowds of 30,000-plus regularly began packing the place, Syracuse did not just have a home, it had a dome.

THE CARRIER DOME, THE LARGEST ON-CAMPUS ARENA IN THE NATION. The Carrier Dome took almost a year and a half to build with construction costs coming to $28 million. The Carrier Corporation offered a $2.7 million gift, hence the name, even though the building has no air conditioning. It covers 7.7 acres. At the center, the dome's roof hovers 160 feet above the floor. The roof, which was replaced in 1999, weighs 220 tons. Its 287,000 square feet of fiberglass are kept aloft by 14, 3-inch thick steel bridge cables and 16, 5-foot diameter fans that pump in enough air pressure to inflate the roof. To combat Syracuse's notorious winters, the fans can bring in air heated to 140 degrees to melt the snow on top of the roof. In the heaviest of snowstorms, the roof can be lowered, melting the snow faster and allowing easier drainage.

FAST EDDIE MOSS. Eddie Moss, shown here with coach Jim Boeheim, possessed some of the fastest hands and feet of any Syracuse player. Moss, who played from 1977 to 1981, used those attributes to become one of the toughest defenders ever to wear Orange. He set a single-season steals record in 1980–1981 with 85 thefts. The record stood until Jason Hart broke it in 1997. On offense, Moss was a play-making point guard, who still ranks fifth in career assists.

THE CARRIER DOME'S DEBUT. The first regular season game at the Carrier Dome brought the Columbia University Lions in to face the Syracuse Orangemen on November 29, 1980. Eddie Moss was the cover boy on that historic game program. The Orangemen easily handled Columbia in a 108-81 romp.

THE ORANGEMEN AND THE HOYAS. In this February 9, 1981 game, the Orangemen defeated Georgetown 66-64 at the Carrier Dome. Shown here on defense for Syracuse, from left to right, are Leo Rautins, Dan Schayes, Erich Santifer, and Eddie Moss. Georgetown's Fred Brown is in the foreground. After Syracuse moved into the Carrier Dome in the 1980–1981 season, the Orangemen played the Hoyas nine times at home in the 1980s. The Hoyas won four times, while Syracuse won five. None of Syracuse's wins were by more than 5 points except for an 82-76 overtime victory in 1989. As the decade got rolling, the annual Syracuse-Georgetown game drew tremendous crowds to the Carrier Dome. From 1983 to 1989, every Syracuse-Georgetown game attracted a crowd of 30,000 or more. Syracuse and Georgetown met eight times in the Big East Tournament during the 1980s. The Orangemen earned a 3-5 record against the Hoyas in the tournament but lost all four championship games. (Photograph by Lawrence Mason Jr.)

ERICH SANTIFER AND MARTY HEADD. Just before the 1981 Big East Tournament, Syracuse senior Marty Headd broke his right wrist. His replacement in the starting lineup was junior Erich Santifer. In this picture, Santifer hugs Headd as the Orangemen close out a 91-76 victory over the University of Michigan in the NIT to advance to the tournament's semifinals. (Photograph by Lawrence Mason Jr.)

DANNY SCHAYES. Danny Schayes rips a rebound away from Villanova's John Pinone in the 1981 Big East Tournament finals. Syracuse out-lasted the Wildcats, winning 83-80 in triple-overtime. Schayes, whose father Dolph played for the Syracuse Nats, went on to have the longest NBA career of any Syracuse player. Schayes spent 18 seasons in the NBA with seven teams, including Utah, Denver, Milwaukee, Los Angeles, Phoenix, Miami, and Orlando. (Photograph by Lawrence Mason Jr.)

SYRACUSE STUNS HOUSTON.
Erich Santifer celebrates
Syracuse's 92-87 victory over
the University of Houston
on December 11, 1982, at
the Carrier Dome. This was
the year of Houston's Phi
Slamma Jamma squad, which
included Clyde Drexler and
Hakeem (then Akeem)
Olajuwon. Houston went on
to the NCAA championship
game where they were upset
by North Carolina State
University. The Orangemen
went 21-10 that season, losing
to Ohio State University
in the second round of the
NCAA Tournament.

RAUTINS REVERSES. Leo Rautins,
shown here flipping in a reverse
lay-up against Providence College,
transferred to Syracuse from the
University of Minnesota and for the
next three years displayed incredible
all-around skills. Rautins and Dale
Shackleford are the only two players
to lead Syracuse in both assists and
rebounds. In 1983, the Philadelphia
76ers selected Rautins with the 17th
pick in that year's draft.

BRUIN GOES VERTICAL. One of the highest-profile recruits in Jim Boeheim's early years at Syracuse was New York native Tony "Red" Bruin, whose leaping ability was legendary. A high-flying forward, Bruin played from 1979 to 1983. Here, Bruin shows off his vertical leap with a stunning dunk over a bewildered Providence Friar. (Photograph by Lizabeth J. Menzies.)

GENE WALDRON. Gene Waldron played for Syracuse from 1980 to 1984, providing steady backcourt play and standout defense during all four years. Waldron led the Orangemen in steals in 1981–1982 and 1982–1983. Even though he never led in assists in a single season, he somehow managed to rank third on Syracuse's all-time list and, today, still ranks eighth with 410 assists.

HOYA PARANOIA. There is no questioning the fact that Syracuse's arch rivals are the Georgetown Hoyas. The proof is in the people. Six of the top 10 crowds in Carrier Dome history came to watch Syracuse play Georgetown. Dave Gavitt, the Big East Conference's first commissioner, and his successor, Mike Tranghese, have both stated that the Georgetown-Syracuse rivalry, particularly those games at the Carrier Dome, helped boost the conference on a national scale. The Carrier Dome's first crowd of more than 30,000 was the 31,327 fans who witnessed a Syracuse-Georgetown tilt on January 10, 1983. Back in those days, the team benches were on the side of the court in front of the blue curtain, forcing opponents to look up at the majority of the crowd. Today, the team benches sit on the sideline opposite the curtain.

RAFAEL ADDISON. From the 1982–1983 season through 1985–1986, Rafael Addison was one of Syracuse's best offensive players. He scored 1,876 points and remains eighth on Syracuse's scoring charts. The Phoenix Suns selected him in the second round of the 1986 draft. He went on to play six years in the NBA in addition to several years in professional leagues overseas.

SPERA SPINS. Sonny Spera, from Union-Endicott High School, was an Orangeman from 1982 to 1985. Never a regular starter, Spera, nonetheless, helped Syracuse move from a regional power to a national program in the early 1980s, along with Leo Rautins, Tony Bruin, Rafael Addison, and a certain guy called "Pearl."

PEARL. Dwayne "Pearl" Washington brought excitement to the Carrier Dome. His arrival in the fall of 1983 coincided with the boom in attendance at games. Washington came from Brooklyn, and his game relied on the flash of the playground. Fans loved Pearl. Campus stores sold T-shirts that read, "On the seventh day, God created Pearl." Despite playing just three years at Syracuse before entering the NBA, Washington ranks third in assists and fourth in steals on the school's career charts.

SUPER SOPHOMORE. After becoming the first freshman ever named first-team All–Big East the previous year, Pearl Washington made the cover of the 1984–1985 Big East basketball yearbook. Washington averaged 14.4 points and 6.2 assists as a freshman. (Photograph courtesy Dr. Stephen Marshall.)

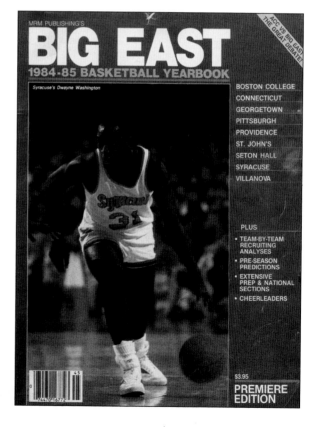

MRM PUBLISHING'S

BIG EAST
1984-85 BASKETBALL YEARBOOK

ACC VS BIG EAST
THE GREAT DEBATE

Syracuse's Dwayne Washington

BOSTON COLLEGE
CONNECTICUT
GEORGETOWN
PITTSBURGH
PROVIDENCE
ST. JOHN'S
SETON HALL
SYRACUSE
VILLANOVA

PLUS

• TEAM-BY-TEAM RECRUITING ANALYSES
• PRE-SEASON PREDICTIONS
• EXTENSIVE PREP & NATIONAL SECTIONS
• CHEERLEADERS

$3.95

PREMIERE EDITION

THE LEGEND OF PEARL. Numbers fall far short of describing the play of Pearl Washington. It was not that he scored 1,490 points in his career; it was the half-court shot that beat Boston College. It was not that he doled out 637 assists in just three years; it was the Big East Tournament record 14 assists he had against St. John's in 1986. It was not that he picked Syracuse; it was that he announced the decision on national television as NBC's Al McGuire interviewed him. He was, simply, Pearl.

PEARL ON THE COVER. Pearl Washington graced the cover of the game program when Syracuse hosted Southern California College on November 29, 1985. This was Washington's final season at Syracuse. He entered the NBA draft after a stellar junior season in which he averaged 17.3 points and 7.8 assists per game while leading the Orangemen to a 26-6 record. (Photograph courtesy Dr. Stephen Marshall.)

93

THE 1987 FINAL FOUR TEAM. In 1987, the Orangemen made it back to the Final Four for the second time in school history and the first time under head coach Jim Boeheim. The Orangemen defeated the University of Florida and the University of North Carolina in the East Region semifinals and finals to advance to New Orleans where they met Big East rival Providence College. After beating the Friars 77-63, Syracuse suffered a heartbreaking 74-73 loss to Indiana University on Keith Smart's game-winning shot. The Syracuse roster included, from left to right, the following: (front row) Herman Harried, Joel Katz, Sherman Douglas, Howard Triche, Greg Monroe, Stephen Thompson, Keith Hughes, and Joey Kohm; (middle row) assistant coach Bernie Fine, head coach Jim Boeheim, Rodney Walker, Derek Brower, Rony Seikaly, Derrick Coleman, Erik Rogers, Matt Roe, assistant coach Wayne Morgan, and assistant coach Barry Copeland; (back row) manager Sam Carello, graduate assistant Matt Bassett, volunteer assistant Ralph Willard, and manager David Lambert.

BOEHEIM WITH THE 1987 CAPTAINS. The starting five on the 1986–1987 Final Four team included three future NBA players in Derrick Coleman, Rony Seikaly, and Sherman Douglas, but the Orangemen leaned heavily on the leadership and experience of senior co-captains Greg Monroe and Howard Triche. Here Monroe (left) and Triche flank head coach Jim Boeheim.

CORCORAN'S HOWARD TRICHE. Howard Triche played his high school ball at Syracuse's Corcoran High School and then went across town to the Syracuse University Hill. Triche, who played at Syracuse from 1984 to 1987, became a co-captain on the 1987 NCAA Final Four team. His defense, rebounding, and leadership (plus the occasional dunk) were crucial to Syracuse's success that season.

WHO SHOT J.R? RONY SEIKALY. Rony Seikaly dominated the University of North Carolina's highly touted J.R. Reid in the 1987 East Regional finals. Seikaly, shown here rising above Reid for 2 points, scored 26 points and owned the boards with 11 rebounds as the Orangemen upset the No. 1-seeded Tar Heels 79-75 at the Meadowlands.

ON TO NEW ORLEANS. The Syracuse Orangemen had just beaten North Carolina to earn a trip to the 1987 Final Four in New Orleans, and the celebrating was just getting started. From left to right, Derrick Coleman, Greg Monroe, and Rony Seikaly enjoy the victory along with CBS announcer Brent Musberger.

BOEHEIM GETS A LIFT AFTER A WIN OVER NORTH CAROLINA. The Syracuse Orangemen defeated North Carolina 79-75 in the NCAA Tournament's East Regional finals, earning the team a spot in the 1987 Final Four and a victory ride for coach Jim Boeheim. Shown here, from left to right, are Stephen Thompson, Rony Seikaly, Matt Roe, Derrick Coleman, Boeheim, Derek Brower, Joel Katz, and Howard Triche. Seikaly scored 26 points, hauled down 11 rebounds against North Carolina, and was named the most valuable player of the East Regionals. Derrick Coleman had 14 rebounds and 8 points. Sherman Douglas scored 14 points as the Orangemen held off the No. 1-seeded Tar Heels and advanced to the Final Four in New Orleans. The win over North Carolina marked Syracuse's first trip to the Final Four since 1975 when Boeheim was an assistant on coach Roy Danforth's staff.

A RALLY AT CITY HALL FOR THE ORANGEMEN. Before leaving Syracuse for the 1987 NCAA Final Four, the Orangemen received a send-off with a pep rally at city hall in downtown Syracuse. Shown here, from left to right, are co-captain Greg Monroe, coach Jim Boeheim, and co-captain Howard Triche.

BOEHEIM AT THE FINAL FOUR. In his 11th season as Syracuse's head coach, Jim Boeheim arrived at the Final Four with his 1986–1987 team. In 11 seasons, his teams won 250 games, made the NCAA Tournament nine times, and the NIT twice. However, the Final Four put Boeheim in the national spotlight.

D.C. FRIES THE FRIARS. Derrick Coleman, then just a freshman, attempts a shot in Syracuse's 77-63 victory over Providence in the 1987 NCAA semifinals. Coleman played a fabulous game against the Friars and scored 12 points, grabbing 12 rebounds, blocking 2 shots, and swiping 2 steals.

POSTING UP PROVIDENCE. Rony Seikaly continued his excellent play in the 1987 postseason in the Final Four against Providence. Seikaly, then a junior, out-muscled the Friars for 16 points and 6 rebounds in Syracuse's 77-63 victory over the Friars. The Orangemen advanced to face Indiana—which had defeated the University of Nevada, Las Vegas, 97-93—in the NCAA championship game.

SEIKALY APPLIES THE DEFENSE. Rony Seikaly stops Indiana's Daryl Thomas during the 1987 championship game. Seikaly averaged 15.1 points, 8.2 rebounds, and 2.1 assists for the Orangemen during the 1986–1987 season.

HOWARD VERSUS THE HOOSIERS. Howard Triche battles an Indiana player for a rebound in the 1987 NCAA championship game. Triche scored Syracuse's last 3 points of the game and hit a short jumper with 57 seconds left to put Syracuse ahead 72-70. He hit 1 out of 2 free throws with 38 seconds remaining for a 73-70 lead. However, Indiana guard Keith Smart scored the game's final 4 points for a 74-73 Hoosiers' win.

THOMPSON TO THE HOOP. Syracuse's Stephen Thompson drives past Indiana's Steve Alford, left, on the way to the basket in the 1987 NCAA title game. A crowd of 64,959 witnessed the game at the Louisiana Superdome in New Orleans. That year, the Orangemen played in the NCAA championship game for the first time in the school's history. Derrick Coleman set a freshman record with 19 rebounds. Sherman Douglas scored 20 points for the Orange, but Indiana guard Keith Smart scored 21 points, including the game-winning jumper with four seconds remaining to give the Hoosiers a 74-73 victory and coach Bob Knight his third national championship.

RONY SEIKALY. Only three players in Syracuse history have led the Orangemen in blocked shots for four consecutive seasons: Roosevelt Bouie, Etan Thomas, and Rony Seikaly who is shown here recording 1 of his 319 career blocks. Seikaly played from 1984 to 1988. As a junior, he started on the 1987 NCAA Final Four team. In the 1988 NBA draft, the Miami Heat selected Seikaly with the No. 9 overall pick. Seikaly's 11-year NBA career ended in 1999. (Photograph by David Grunfield.)

THE "HELICOPTER." Herman Harried carried the nickname the "Helicopter" with him when he came to Syracuse from Baltimore powerhouse Dunbar High School. Despite standing six feet nine inches tall, Harried had such amazing jumping ability that he seemed to hang in the air. A devastating knee injury in his sophomore year took away a lot of Harried's athleticism. However, he remained a fan favorite and, today, is a high school coach at Baltimore's Lake Clifton High School.

GENERAL SHERMAN. Sherman Douglas ran Syracuse's offense like a true floor general. As a sophomore, he led the Orangemen to the 1987 NCAA title game. He threw the lob pass better than anybody. His football-style hike to Stevie Thompson against Indiana in the 1988 Big Apple NIT remains a highlight-reel classic. His 960 career assists were an NCAA record at the time and still stand as a school record. He still shares the NCAA record for most assists in a game with 22 against Providence on January 28, 1989.

SHERMAN DOUGLAS. Douglas, who played at Syracuse from 1986 to 1989, took over the point guard position after Pearl Washington's early departure. Because of his many records for assists, plus the fact that he shared the court with the likes of Derrick Coleman, Stephen Thompson, and Billy Owens, Douglas's offense is often overlooked. However, he was the leading scorer on the 1987 Final Four team, and he led the Orange in scoring as a senior as well. He is one of only four Syracuse players with more than 2,000 career points.

DERRICK COLEMAN. The best player in Syracuse history prior to World War II was Vic Hanson. After him, there was Dave Bing. Derrick Coleman got serious consideration as the best to play at Syracuse since Bing. Coleman is Syracuse's all-time leading rebounder. He ended his career as the school's No. 1 scorer and remains second behind Lawrence Moten despite never leading the Orangemen in scoring in a single season. He is also third in blocked shots. He took the Orangemen to four straight NCAA Tournaments, including the 1987 Final Four where he set an NCAA record with 19 rebounds in the finals against Indiana. In the 1990 NBA draft, the New Jersey Nets used the No. 1 overall pick to select Coleman. Previously, the highest any Syracuse player had gone in the NBA draft was when the Detroit Pistons took Bing with the second pick in the 1966 draft.

STEVIE THOMPSON. For every Sherman Douglas "alley," there was a Stevie Thompson "oop." Thompson, listed at six feet four inches but likely two inches shorter, provided the highlight-reel crescendo to many of Douglas's lob passes. Thompson scored 1,956 points in his college career, and even though he never led the Orangemen in scoring in any of his four years, he still ranks fifth on the university's career scoring list.

COLEMAN AND THOMPSON. Stephen Thompson (left) and Derrick Coleman (right) were two of the most successful players in Syracuse history. Coleman is still the school's all-time leading rebounder; he is second on the scoring list while Thompson is fifth. More importantly, though, their teams won 113 games and lost just 31 from 1986 to 1990. The Orangemen finished first in the Big East twice, appeared in the Big East Tournament finals four times, won the 1988 conference tournament, and went 11-4 in NCAA Tournament play.

BILLY OWENS. Billy Owens appeared on the cover of *Sports Illustrated* before he played in his first game at Syracuse. Owens played at Syracuse for three years before leaving after his junior year to enter the NBA draft where he was the third overall pick. As a freshman, Owens started on the 1988–1989 team that fell one game shy of the Final Four. In this photograph, Owens posts up Missouri's Doug Smith in the 1989 NCAA Midwest Region semifinals. After deferring to Sherman Douglas, Derrick Coleman, and Stephen Thompson in his rookie year, Owens led the Orangemen in scoring as a sophomore even though Coleman and Thompson were seniors on that team. As a junior, Owens averaged 23.3 points per game, more than any Syracuse player since Dave Bing's 28.4 average as a senior in 1966. Owens remains 10th on Syracuse's all-time scoring list and 2nd only to Bing for players with three years of varsity competition.

OWENS RIPS DOWN A REBOUND.
Billy Owens was a multi-talented
player. At six feet nine inches tall,
he played both forward positions
in his three-year college career. He
could shoot with either hand. He
could also handle the ball like a
guard, but Owens was an underrated
rebounder. Owens, who ranks
seventh among the university's
career rebound leaders, averaged
11.6 rebounds as a junior in 1991.
No Orangemen has come within
two rebounds of that figure since.

THE UNSTOPPABLE FORCE. Had
he stayed for his senior year, Billy
Owens probably would have set a
record for scoring that might have
stood forever. Owens, shown here
attempting a shot over Duke's Alaa
Abdelnaby in the 1989–1990 season,
scored 1,840 points in three years. As
a junior, he scored 744 points. If he
had repeated that kind of season as
a senior, Owens would have tallied
more than 2,500 points. Lawrence
Moten holds the school scoring
record with 2,334 points.

THE DOME THRONG WATCHES THE ORANGE BEAT THE HUSKIES. On February 10, 1990, the Orangemen defeated the University of Connecticut 90-86 in front of a crowd of 32,820 in the Carrier Dome. Here, Derrick Coleman inbounds the ball to Billy Owens. The crowd remains the fourth largest in Carrier Dome history and the largest for any Syracuse opponent not named Georgetown. The Orangemen averaged 29,919 fans for its 16 home games in the 1989–1990 season, setting an NCAA record that still stands. The Orangemen won the Big East Conference regular season crown, however, Connecticut later avenged the Carrier Dome loss with a 78-75 win over Syracuse in the Big East Tournament's championship game. The Orangemen eventually lost to Minnesota in the NCAA Midwest Region semifinals.

THE ORANGEMEN CELEBRATE THE BIG EAST TOURNEY TITLE. After Billy Owens left Syracuse University with one year of eligibility remaining to enter the 1991 NBA draft, expectations were relatively low for the Orangemen the following season. Dave Johnson, Mike Hopkins, and Dave Siock were the team's veterans. Adrian Autry was a returning starter. Those Orangemen showed remarkable pluck and finished with a 22-10 record. The Orangemen kept alive a 10-year streak of NCAA Tournament appearances. In the tournament, Syracuse beat Princeton and then lost to the University of Massachusetts, Amherst, 77-71 in overtime. The season's highlight came with a 56-54 victory over Georgetown to capture the Big East Tournament crown, which was Syracuse's first since 1988. From left to right, Michael Edwards, Anthony Harris, Mike Hopkins, Dave Johnson, Conrad McRae, Lawrence Moten, Scott McCorkle, and Adrian Autry celebrate the championship.

THE LATE CONRAD MCRAE. In July 2000, former Syracuse University player Conrad McRae died of apparent heart failure during practice with the Orlando Magic's summer-league team in Los Angeles. McRae played at Syracuse from 1990 to 1993. He had an enthusiastic and fun-loving personality, which was personified by his passionate dunks. His death stunned the Syracuse community. Dozens of university teammates turned out for the funeral in his hometown of Brooklyn.

ADRIAN "RED" AUTRY. One of only three players to lead the Orangemen in assists for four years, Adrian Autry ranks fourth all-time in assists and fifth in steals. In his last game for Syracuse, Autry scored all 31 of his points after halftime in the 1994 NCAA Sweet 16 game against Missouri. Autry's heroics were not enough, and the Orange lost 98-88 in overtime. (Photograph courtesy Dr. Stephen Marshall.)

HOPKINS AND MOTEN ON THE BREAK. The 1992–1993 Syracuse squad had seemingly little to play for. The Orangemen knew going into the season that they would not be eligible for postseason play because of the NCAA's sanctions against the program. Players such as Mike Hopkins and Lawrence Moten, who exemplified the character of that year's team, helped the Orangemen to a 20-9 record and a spot in the Big East Tournament's championship game.

TEACHER AND STUDENT. Whatever Jim Boeheim is telling Mike Hopkins in this photograph, Hopkins must have listened. Hopkins, a lightly regarded recruit, played at Syracuse from 1989 to 1993. Through hard work and desire, he turned himself into a two-year starter. In 1995, Hopkins returned to his alma mater as a member of Boeheim's coaching staff.

SYRACUSE'S ALL-TIME LEADING SCORER. He arrived without the ballyhoo of most big-time recruits, but four years later Lawrence Moten left Syracuse with more career points than any player in school history. Moten, shown here soaring in for a dunk against Villanova in 1994, played from 1991 to 1995. He scored 2,334 points at Syracuse, finishing his career with a 19.3 scoring average. He scored 18.2 points per game as a freshman to set another school record. He is also the Big East's career scoring leader with 1,405 points in conference games. Many observers, including Jim Boeheim, credit Moten with keeping the Syracuse basketball program at a high level in the wake of the NCAA's investigation and the one-year probation imposed in the 1992–1993 season.

POETRY IN MOTEN. Lawrence Moten earned the nickname "Poetry in Moten" with his silky, smooth moves. Moten, a six-foot-five-inch tall guard, was especially adept at finding ways to score close to the basket. In this photograph, Moten takes the ball right at Georgetown center Othella Harrington for a basket and a foul.

MOTEN LEADS SYRACUSE AGAINST MISSOURI. Lawrence Moten scored 29 points against Missouri in the Sweet 16 of the 1994 NCAA Tournament, but the Orangemen lost to the Tigers 98-88 in overtime. Moten's performance against Missouri continued a stellar NCAA Tournament for the junior. Moten scored 29 points in a first-round victory over Hawaii and came back with 17 points in the second round against the University of Wisconsin, Green Bay.

JOHN WALLACE. Two years after Derrick Coleman left Syracuse, a new No. 44 arrived on the scene. John Wallace, a native of Rochester, New York, lived up to the number's legacy. Wallace led Syracuse in rebounding for four consecutive seasons, joining Coleman as the only players to accomplish that feat. In his senior year, Wallace turned up the offense, scoring 22.2 points per game for a Final Four-bound team. His 22.2 points per game are second only to Billy Owens's 23.3 in 1990–1991 during the Jim Boeheim era. After the 1996 Final Four, the New York Knicks took Wallace with the 18th overall pick in that year's NBA draft. In the six years since, Wallace has played for the Knicks, the Toronto Raptors, the Detroit Pistons, and the Phoenix Suns. Wallace and Coleman are the only players who rank in Syracuse's top five for scoring, rebounding, and blocked shots.

Seven

The Cuse Is in the House

THE ROAD TO THE FINAL FOUR. The Syracuse Orangemen celebrate their 60-57 upset of heavily favored Kansas in the finals of the 1996 NCAA West Regional in Denver. The victory advanced Syracuse to its third Final Four. The Orangemen captivated basketball fans around the country and especially in central New York with their theme song "The Cuse is in the House!"

WALLACE STUNS GEORGIA. John Wallace leans in for a shot against Georgia in the 1996 West Region semifinals in Denver. Wallace came through twice for the Orangemen in their 83-81 overtime victory. His football-style inbounds pass from half-court set up Jason Cipolla's game-tying shot at the end of regulation, and then he won the game with a 3-pointer with two seconds remaining in overtime.

HILL ROCKS THE JAYHAWKS. In the 1996 West Region final, Otis Hill out-played two future NBA players to lead Syracuse to a 60-57 win over Kansas. Hill, shown here attempting a shot over Kansas's Paul Pierce and Raef LaFrentz, scored 15 points and pulled down 6 rebounds compared to a total of 16 points and 16 rebounds from Kansas centers LaFrentz and Scot Pollard.

THE 1996 NCAA FINALISTS. The 1995–1996 Orangemen entered the NCAA Tournament with a 24-8 record and a No. 4 seed in the West Region. Syracuse put on a remarkable run through the tournament, stunning Georgia in overtime and then upsetting Kansas to earn the school's third Final Four appearance. The Orangemen advanced to the championship game with a semifinal win over Mississippi State. Syracuse lost to Kentucky in the finals. The team consisted of these men, from left to right: (front row) Todd Burgan, Otis Hill, John Wallace, Lazarus Sims, Jim Hayes, Elimu Nelson, and J.B. Reafsnyder; (middle row) David Patrick, Jason Cipolla, Bobby Lazor, Elvir Ovcina, Marius Janulis, and James May; (back row) head manager Mike Scherban, graduate assistant Todd Blumen, assistant coach Mike Hopkins, assistant coach Bernie Fine, head coach Jim Boeheim, assistant coach Wayne Morgan, administrative assistant Jeff Estis, manager Tara Russo, and manager David Schapiro.

THE ORANGEMEN MEET THE PRESS. Press conferences are a big part of any Final Four. At the 1996 Final Four, the underdog Orangemen were the subjects of intense media coverage. At this Final Four press conference, Syracuse was represented by, from left to right, Jason Cipolla, Todd Burgan, head coach Jim Boeheim, Lazarus Sims, John Wallace, and Otis Hill.

BURGAN SLAMS STATE. Todd Burgan's alley-oop dunk was just 2 of his 19 points in Syracuse's victory over Mississippi State University in the semifinals of the 1996 Final Four. Burgan made 6 of 11 field goal attempts and went 6 for 7 at the free throw line. Burgan, just a sophomore, also hauled in 7 rebounds against the Bulldogs.

WALLACE AND SIMS AFTER THE FINAL FOUR WIN. John Wallace and Lazarus Sims, Syracuse's senior co-captains, share an embrace after the Orangemen defeated Mississippi State University 77-69 in the 1996 Final Four at the Meadowlands in East Rutherford, New Jersey. Wallace led the Orangemen with 21 points against Mississippi State. Sims scored 11 points, picked up 5 rebounds, handed out 9 assists, and committed not a single turnover. The two seniors were the heart and soul of the 1996 team. Wallace led Syracuse in both scoring and rebounding. Sims recorded 281 assists, more than any Syracuse player other than Sherman Douglas. In the semifinal win over the Bulldogs, Wallace and Sims were the only Syracuse players to play the game's entire 40 minutes. The victory put Syracuse, an upstart No. 4 seed, into the NCAA championship game against the University of Kentucky.

WALLACE GOES OVER WALKER. In the 1996 NCAA championship game, Syracuse's John Wallace, shown here taking a shot over the University of Kentucky's Antoine Walker, almost carried the Orangemen to a title. Wallace scored a game-high 29 points and also hauled in 10 rebounds before fouling out of the game.

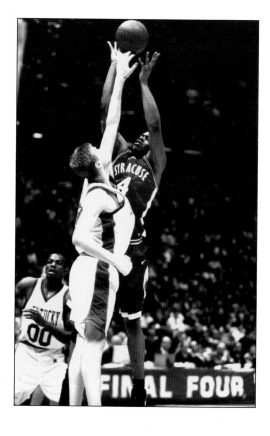

OTIS HILL SHOOTS AGAINST KENTUCKY. Syracuse center Otis Hill attempts a shot against Kentucky's Mark Pope in the 1996 NCAA championship game. The underdog Orangemen lost to the Wildcats 76-67. Hill scored 9 points. He also held Kentucky centers Walter McCarty and Mark Pope to a combined 8 points in the title game.

BURGAN TAKES ON THE CATS. Most Syracuse fans remember John Wallace's terrific performance in the 1996 title game against the University of Kentucky, but sophomore Todd Burgan also had a terrific game. Burgan scored 19 points on 7 for 10 shooting and challenged the Wildcats for 8 rebounds before fouling out after playing 38 minutes. Burgan earned All-Tournament honors along with Wallace.

SIMS AVOIDS TROUBLE. Lazarus Sims spins away from a Kentucky defender as Syracuse's Todd Burgan (No. 30) and Syracuse coach Jim Boeheim give him room. Sims played a critical role in Syracuse's efforts against Kentucky's full-court-press defense. He scored just six points, but dished out seven assists despite the Wildcats' pressure.

SYRACUSE ALUMNI CHEER ON THE ORANGE. When Syracuse made it to the 1996 Final Four, the alumni turned out in force. Some of the more famous graduates included Derrick Coleman (1986 to 1990; left) and Lawrence Moten (1991 to 1995; right). Coleman is Syracuse's all-time leading rebounder and second leading scorer. Moten is the school's all-time leading scorer.

McNABB TRADES GRIDIRON FOR HARDWOOD. Donovan McNabb, an All-America quarterback, joined the Syracuse University basketball team for the 1995–1996 and 1996–1997 seasons. This photograph was taken during McNabb's biggest game in a Syracuse University basketball uniform. In a 1997 game against Georgetown at the Carrier Dome, McNabb rescued the foul-plagued Orangemen by coming off the bench for 10 points and 6 rebounds. McNabb's energy and fearlessness led the Orangemen to a 77-74 victory over the Hoyas.

THE ALL-ALUMNI COACHING STAFF. When former Syracuse player Louis Orr returned to his alma mater in 1996–1997 as an assistant coach, the coaching staff consisted entirely of Syracuse alumni. Shown, from left to right, are assistant coach Mike Hopkins (Class of 1993), assistant coach Bernie Fine (Class of 1967), head coach Jim Boeheim (Class of 1966), and Orr (Class of 1980).

BERNIE FINE. A member of Jim Boeheim's coaching staff right from the beginning, Syracuse University assistant coach Bernie Fine has earned a reputation for developing centers including Danny Schayes, Rony Seikaly, and Etan Thomas. Fine, shown here counseling Thomas, served as the team's manager during his years as an undergraduate at Syracuse. He was the head coach at Syracuse's Henninger High School when Boeheim hired him in 1976.

ETAN ERASES ANOTHER SHOT. Etan Thomas, the most prolific shot-blocker in Syracuse history, swats away an attempt by University of Connecticut's Rashamel Jones in a 1999 game at the Carrier Dome. Thomas racked up 424 rejections in his career, almost 100 more than Roosevelt Bouie, the previous record-holder. Thomas ranks second all-time in the Big East for blocks behind Georgetown great Patrick Ewing.

JASON HART. Jason Hart did more than just break Sherman Douglas's school record for career steals, he shattered it. Hart finished his career with 329 steals, 94 more than Douglas. He broke Douglas's old record in his junior year. Hart became the first Syracuse player to lead the team in steals four straight years.

JANULIS DEFLATES GAELS. Marius Janulis's three-point basket with 1.2 seconds remaining turned back Iona College's upset bid in the first round of the 1998 NCAA Tournament in Lexington, Kentucky. The Iona Gaels, coached by former Syracuse assistant Tim Welsh, appeared to have victory in hand when Todd Burgan's late drive was thwarted. But Burgan recovered the ball and threw it to Janulis, who canned the game-winner.

HART AND JANULIS CELEBRATE. Jason Hart jumps into Marius Janulis's arms after Janulis's 3-pointer put the Orangemen ahead of Iona 63-61, with 1.2 seconds remaining in a first-round game in the 1998 NCAA Tournament's South Regional. The Orangemen went on to whip the University of New Mexico 56-46 in the second round before losing to Duke 80-67 in the Sweet 16.

THE CARRIER DOME LOCKER ROOM. With thousands in the Carrier Dome's arena waiting to cheer them on, this is where the Syracuse players receive their final instructions. The players' lockers are painted orange with their portraits displayed on top. Large action photographs adorn other portions of the locker room.

OTTO THE ORANGE. Otto the Orange had been around for almost 15 years before finally becoming the university's official mascot in 1995 after fending off an attempt to find a new mascot. Otto first emerged in the early 1980s, just a few years after the university mothballed the Saltine Warrior. The Saltine Warrior, a student in a Native American costume, made his first appearance in the early 1950s. In 1978, a member of a Native American student organization led a protest against using the Saltine Warrior as a mascot. In the years since, Otto, a television commercial icon, has become nationally recognized as the singular Syracuse University mascot.

THE ALL-CENTURY TEAM. In 2000, Syracuse University invited fans to help select an All-Century team. On February 17, 2000, the players were honored during a halftime ceremony. On hand were, from left to right, the following: (front row) unidentified sponsor, Greg Kohls, Billy Gabor, Jim Lee, Dennis DuVal, Sherman Douglas, and Dwayne "Pearl" Washington; (back row) unidentified sponsor, Vinnie Cohen, Dave Bing, Marty Byrnes, Roosevelt Bouie, Rafael Addison, and Rony Seikaly. Orangemen Jason Hart and Etan Thomas along with assistant Louis Orr and head coach and All-Century coach Jim Boeheim were in the locker room during the halftime presentation. Others on the 25-player team were Derrick Coleman, Rudy Hackett, Vic Hanson, Lawrence Moten, Billy Owens, Leo Rautins, Danny Schayes, Joseph Schwarzer, Stephen Thompson, and John Wallace.

JIM BOEHEIM COURT. On February 24, 2002, Syracuse University officials dedicated the Carrier Dome court in honor of Jim Boeheim. A Syracuse University graduate, former player, assistant coach, and 26-year head coach, Boeheim enjoyed the moment with his wife Juli and his children. With 623 wins and just 221 losses in his 26 seasons, Boeheim's .738 winning percentage currently ranks 3rd among active Division I coaches, behind only Kansas's Roy Williams and Utah's Rick Majerus. He is 10th among active coaches in career victories. Boeheim took Syracuse, an Eastern power in the 1970s, and turned it into a national program. He guided the Orangemen into the Big East Conference. Syracuse has seven regular season Big East championships and three tournament titles. Boeheim, the Big East's lone remaining original coach, has won the league's coach-of-the-year award three times.

Eight

NATIONAL CHAMPIONS

SYRACUSE CELEBRATES. The 2003 Syracuse Orangemen celebrate their 81-78 victory over Kansas in the NCAA championship game at the Louisiana Superdome in New Orleans. The shoes at the bottom with the toes pointing up belong to Syracuse freshman Carmelo Anthony, who scored 20 points, grabbed 10 rebounds, and dished out 7 assists in the championship game.

CARMELO ANTHONY. Carmelo Anthony came to Syracuse University with great expectations heaped upon him. He exceeded all of them. Anthony, a six-foot-eight-inch forward from Baltimore, was the first McDonald's All-American to play for Syracuse since John Wallace, who played from 1992 to 1996. In his college debut, Anthony scored 27 points against Memphis at Madison Square Garden. He scored at least 20 points in each of his first nine games. In every game he scored at least 10 points, and he had 22 games in which he reached double figures in both points and rebounds. Eventually, he set school records for a freshman in scoring (22.2 points per game) and rebounding (10 per game). He was named the Big East Conference's Rookie of the Week 10 times, breaking former Georgetown star Allen Iverson's record of nine. Anthony made first-team All–Big East, becoming just the second freshman in league history to do so. The other was former Syracuse star Dwayne "Pearl" Washington. At season's end, Anthony was the consensus national Freshman of the Year and earned first-team All-America honors from the *Sporting News*.

130

KUETH DUANY. Kueth Duany, a six-foot-six-inch guard from Bloomington, Indiana, was the only senior on the 2002–2003 team. Duany provided leadership on and off the court. He also proved a fierce defender and an effective offensive player. He was a vital cog in the team's success. At the Big East tournament, Duany was named the conference's Sportsman of the Year, an award that recognized his leadership and hustle.

MATT GORMAN. Matt Gorman, a six-foot-nine-inch forward from Watertown, New York, played in nine games as a freshman. A gifted shooter who gained strength in his first year at Syracuse, Gorman averaged just 2.3 points and 2.1 rebounds per game. However, his practice contributions in battles with veterans Craig Forth, Jeremy McNeil, and Hakim Warrick were immeasurable.

131

JEREMY MCNEIL. Jeremy McNeil did not start a single game in the 2002–2003 season. He averaged just 3.3 points per game. But the Syracuse Orangemen owe much of their national championship to the muscular center from San Antonio. Trailing Oklahoma State by 17 points in the second round of the NCAA Tournament, Syracuse went to a full-court pressing defense. Whenever Oklahoma State broke the press, McNeil was there to turn the Cowboys away with an awe-inspiring block. His presence changed the game. In all, McNeil recorded four blocks and seven rebounds against Oklahoma State.

JOSH PACE. Josh Pace, a six-foot-five-inch guard-forward, became the ultimate role player for the Orangemen in his sophomore year. Pace averaged 4.3 points and 2.7 rebounds per game, but when the Orange needed him, Pace always seemed to rise to the occasion. He reached double figures just three times in the regular season, but he scored 14 points against Auburn in the NCAA's Sweet 16 and then added 12- and 8-point games against Texas and Kansas at the Final Four.

Anthony Buries a Jumper. Carmelo Anthony releases a jump shot in a game against North Carolina-Greensboro for two of his record-setting 778 points as a freshman. Only two Syracuse players ever have scored more than Anthony did in 2002–2003: John Wallace, who had 845 as a senior, and Dave Bing, who had 794 as a senior. Anthony and Gerry McNamara formed the highest-scoring freshmen duo in the country.

Gerry McNamara. Gerry McNamara won over Syracuse fans quickly as a freshman. McNamara staged his coming-out party in this early season game against Georgia Tech, scoring 25 points and hitting 5 out of 12 attempts from 3-point range. Only Preston Shumpert made more 3-pointers in a season than McNamara's 85 treys in 2002–2003.

Hakim Warrick. Hakim Warrick slammed the opposition in 2002–2003. The six-foot-eight-inch forward with the pogo-stick legs recorded 80 dunks as a sophomore, almost three times as many as any of his Syracuse teammates (Jeremy McNeil had 31). Warrick electrified the Carrier Dome with his gravity-defying slams. But Warrick did more than dunk. He averaged 14.8 points and 8.5 rebounds per game, both big increases over his numbers as a freshman, to earn the Big East Most Improved Player award.

THE CARRIER DOME ROCKS AGAIN. As the 2002–2003 season began to take on a special feel, the crowds at the Carrier Dome began to swell to late-1980s proportions. On the first of February, 30,303 fans came to see Syracuse face Pittsburgh, the nation's second-ranked team. A win would vault the Panthers into the No. 1 position. The crowd was the largest at the Carrier Dome in three years. The Orangemen did not disappoint. Jeremy McNeil scored all four of his points in the game's final minute, including a follow-up basket with three seconds left that gave Syracuse a 67-65 lead. It was Syracuse's first victory against a team ranked second in the nation since 1989, when the Orangemen defeated Georgetown 82-76 in overtime. By the season's end, though, the attendance mark for the Syracuse-Pittsburgh game had been eclipsed twice. Syracuse's game against Notre Dame attracted 32,116 fans. In the regular-season finale, Syracuse set an NCAA on-campus record as 33,071 fans crammed the Carrier Dome to see Syracuse take on Rutgers and to be there for Carmelo Anthony's last home game as an Orangeman.

BOEHEIM IN THE NCAA TOURNAMENT.
Syracuse went 24-5 in the regular season to
earn the school's 22nd NCAA Tournament
bid in Jim Boeheim's 27 seasons as head
coach. Boeheim, shown here in first-round
action against Manhattan, has guided
Syracuse to 38 wins in the NCAA
Tournament, the fourth-highest total of any
active coach and the seventh all-time total.

BOEHEIM POSTGAME.
Syracuse coach
Jim Boeheim smiles
during the postgame
press conference after
the Orangemen's
76-65 win over
Manhattan in
the first round of
the 2003 NCAA
Tournament. Under
Boeheim, Syracuse
is 19-3 in first-round
games with an overall
tournament record of
38-21. Since 1987,
the year of Syracuse's
first Final Four in
Boeheim's era, the
Orangemen are 31-13
in the tournament.

BILLY EDELIN. Billy Edelin made his Syracuse University debut a year and a half later than expected, but he made his time count when the Orangemen started making their NCAA Tournament run. Edelin missed the entire 2001–2002 season due to a university-imposed suspension. He then sat out the first 12 games of the 2002–2003 season as a result of an NCAA rules violation. Edelin averaged 9 points and 2.5 assists in the last 23 games of the season. He never settled into a fixed role, as his minutes rose and fell from game to game. However, Edelin played a huge role in the postseason. He scored 15 points in 29 minutes in Syracuse's first-round victory over Manhattan. Two days later, he scored 20 points to spark Syracuse's comeback win over Oklahoma State. In the six NCAA Tournament games, he averaged 11 points, 3.8 rebounds, and 2.6 assists and made 53.7 percent of his field goal attempts.

McNamara's Band. Gerry McNamara cemented his status as a hero in both Syracuse and his hometown of Scranton, Pennsylvania, with some memorable performances in the NCAA Tournament. McNamara, taking a shot against Oklahoma in the East Regional finals, averaged 13.3 points in the tournament. In the Final Four, he scored 19 and 18 points against Texas and Kansas, respectively.

"Hak" Attacks the Sooners. Hakim Warrick turns for a shot in the East Regional finals against Oklahoma. Warrick scored 13 points on 6-for-9 shooting and also pulled in 9 rebounds in Syracuse's 63-47 throttling of the Sooners. He was named to the all-regional team. After suffering from the flu in the first two rounds, Warrick made 20 out of 36 field goal attempts in Syracuse's next four games.

ON TO THE FINAL FOUR. Carmelo Anthony celebrates Syracuse's 63-47 win over Oklahoma in the finals of the NCAA's East Regional at the Pepsi Center in Albany. The victory vaulted the Orangemen into the 2003 Final Four in New Orleans. Anthony was named the East Regional Most Valuable Player following his 20-point, 10-rebound game against Oklahoma. Anthony rose to the occasion in the regional finals, playing the entire game, something he did just four times all season. In addition to Anthony's play, the story of the East Regional was Syracuse's zone defense. The Orangemen stymied Oklahoma's offense, holding the Sooners to 31 percent shooting and forcing 19 turnovers. The Sooners scored just 20 first-half points. Oklahoma managed just four points in the last nine minutes of the first half. The Sooners' 47 points were 24 points under their season average.

BOEHEIM AND SONS. After Syracuse defeated Oklahoma in the East Regional final at the Pepsi Center in Albany, coach Jim Boeheim enjoyed the moment with his two sons. In Boeheim's arms is Jack, and Jimmy is at his side. Both boys are wearing jerseys with the No. 13, which their father wore during his playing days at Syracuse. The victory over the No. 1-seeded Sooners put the Orangemen in the Final Four for the third time in Boeheim's 27-year head-coaching tenure. This Final Four returned Boeheim to the site of his first Final Four experience, New Orleans, where the Orangemen lost to Indiana in the 1987 NCAA championship game. This time, the Orangemen faced Texas in the semifinals, and Marquette played Kansas in the other game.

CRAIG FORTH HOOKS A HORN. In Syracuse's NCAA semifinal match-up against Texas, center Craig Forth had to battle Texas big men, including Brad Buckman. Forth, a seven-foot sophomore, finished with two points and four rebounds in 21 minutes. Two nights later, Forth came up big against Kansas, contributing six points, three rebounds, and three blocks in 24 minutes of action.

DUANY ATTACKS THE JAYHAWKS.
Syracuse senior Kueth Duany looks over the Kansas defense in the 2003 NCAA championship game. Duany scored 11 points and finished with 4 rebounds against the Jayhawks. Duany's double-figure scoring effort was significant. He scored at least 10 points in 23 games as a senior, and the Orangemen went 22-1 in those games.

ANTHONY LEADS THE ORANGE TO THE TITLE. In the NCAA championship game, Carmelo Anthony turned in one his finest all-around performances of the season. He scored 20 points, grabbed 10 rebounds, and doled out a season-high 7 assists to lead the Orangemen over Kansas. He became just the third freshman to be named Most Outstanding Player of a Final Four, joining Utah's Arnie Ferrin (1944) and Louisville's Pervis Ellison (1986).

ANTHONY AND BOEHEIM ACCEPT THE TROPHY. Syracuse coach Jim Boeheim and star freshman Carmelo Anthony receive the national championship trophy from NCAA president Myles Brand (second from the right). For Boeheim, the 2003 title made up for near misses in 1987 and 1996. In 1987, Boeheim took Syracuse to the Final Four for the first time in his coaching career. The Orangemen lost to Indiana on a last-second shot. That game, coincidentally, was played at the Louisiana Superdome, which was the site of the 2003 Final Four. In 1996, Boeheim got back to the Final Four for a second time, but the Orangemen lost to Kentucky, which was coached by former Boeheim assistant Rick Pitino.

A CHAMPIONSHIP TO CHERISH. Kueth Duany, the Syracuse captain and the only scholarship senior on the team's roster, hugs the NCAA championship trophy in the locker room after the Orangemen's 81-78 victory over Kansas. Making the fourth Final Four appearance in school history, the 2002–2003 Orangemen claimed Syracuse's first NCAA championship. They had lost in the 1975 semifinals and the finals in both 1987 and 1996. Now, they stood alone atop the college basketball world. In their last three games, the Orangemen defeated the No. 1 seed in the East (Oklahoma), the No. 1 seed in the South (Texas), and the No. 2 seed in the West (Kansas). When they returned to Syracuse, a crowd of more than 25,000 packed the Carrier Dome to celebrate the national championship with them.